TUNNEL TALES
OF OUR HEROIC TUNNEL RATS IN VIETNAM

By Robert F. Burgess

Spyglass Publications
Chattahoochee, Florida

TUNNEL TALES OF OUR HEROIC TUNNEL RATS IN VIETNAM

By Robert F. Burgess

SPYGLASS PUBLICATIONS, FLORIDA
All Rights Reserved © 2019 Robert F. Burgess

A 2019 paperback edition

Published by Robert F. Burgess

For information address:

Robert F. Burgess
Spyglass Publications
308 West Marion Street
Chattahoochee, Florida 32324

Cover Design © Robert F. Burgess

Author photo by Charles Harnage Jr.

This book is warmly dedicated to the bravest of the brave, the Tunnel Rats of Vietnam; and to all who were involved in that terrible conflict. You all are our heroes. As long as we remember what heroic things were done there, and these sacrifices continue to be read about in books like this, our heroes will live forever. Their deeds will never be forgotten. God bless you all.

TABLE OF CONTENTS

Foreword

These true Vietnam War tunnel stories first appeared as Amazon Kindle e-books. They quickly received 110 reader reviews that were incredibly heart-warming. Some readers commented that they wished the books to be longer. This collection fulfills that request. I hope reviewers like the result. Here are some of their e-book comments:

Walter Pytlewski wrote, *"Chilling to say the least. We owe a great debt to the soldiers that fought and took great risks everyday in Vietnam. As a Vietnam War vet myself, I still feel we did our jobs and got absolutely no credit for our service. I feel this big hole in my heart that won't heal. I have filled most of the hole with a North Vietnamese wife. In my small way I try, every day, to apologize for our big mistake. The people of the North are really nice to me and very forgiving. The stories they tell me, which never get told, just raises the hair on the back of my neck. We were soldiers on both sides, then there is the population we tried to bomb back to the stone ages. Read the real history of Vietnam and then you will understand why they fought so hard.*

Let's not forget the Agent Orange story that still surfaces in Vietnam today and in the survivors that served there. So many have died of cancer and our government still argues the facts."

One reader wrote: *"If you ever wanted to know about the underground war in Vietnam this is the book to read. Some of the smallest and bravest heroes of their generation, determined to save American lives."*

Another said, *"As a Vietnam Vet, my respect for these brave men is impossible to express. The author's description of events and added humor made for enjoyable and heart felt reading."*

"This short book was a great read. There is none of the long buildup to the actual deployment (growing up etc), it gets right into the "action." The things these brave men went through are unbelievable and makes for an exciting experience. So glad I bought the book."

"No one really understands what these brave men endured. This little book is big in it's telling of the unknown story of these brave men. THANK YOU!"

"I learned a lot about the tunnels that I didn't know. I'm looking for more stories of the tunnel rats. Even more interesting was the life of the enemy in the tunnels. Incredible what they endured."

Young57 wrote: *"I selected this book because of a recent conversation with my sister. She had a talk with our father (in late stages of Alzheimer's) and he told her exactly what his main job was in Nam - tunnel rat. He told me of legendary people like Mad Dog Shriver, Billy Waugh, and Robert Howard; but never told me what he actually did.*

"This book explains so much about the very changed man who returned from his second Nam tour determined to get out ASAP. A man who lived, breathed, and slept Army. I can't wait to get some hard copies of this to send to my sister, perhaps even my mom.

Thank you, Mr. Burgess."

I managed to contact this reader and sent him a printable copy of this book dedicated to his father. He was in Saudi Arabia and planned to print the book for his father who wasn't expected to live beyond his next birthday. I never heard how it turned out.

Be careful reading this book. As described in the author's bio, Bob likes to get the reader involved in the action. So, when he has you gear up with a .45 handgun and crawl head-first into a black-as-ink possibly booby-trapped enemy tunnel, remember that he will be right there behind you every inch of the way. But as you read this it might be smart to put on your rented flak jacket. Just in case!

TUNNEL TALES OF VIETNAM

1

Rule One:
Never Volunteer for Anything
(Unless You Really Want It)

Vietnam 1968

In his unforgettable memoir, Beneath the Bamboo: A Vietnam War Story, *author Jonathan Jones tells us the way it was right from the very beginning. What made him that way and what got him where he was is told as straight forward as possible. His words reflect the uncertainties so many other young men experienced in much the same way as he did, especially when they came in country. Unbeknownst to Jonathan, however, his being small and light-weight was just what was required for one of the most dangerous jobs in the war, that of a Tunnel Rat. How his buddies must have hated the fact that they were physically too big for this special job of crawling through pitch-black tunnels where death might be waiting around every corner, but I guess that's the breaks. Someone had to do it and the little guy lucked right into it. So here, in my words, is what happened to this incredibly brave teenager at that critical time when we were in one very strange nightmarish war in a country far, far away ...*

He was short; there were no two ways about that. A little over five feet. When they sent him to Nam all the guys in his outfit called each other by their nicknames. Between them the CO was called "The Old Man," but that was because he was old and experienced and they really liked him like their own Old Man. Their highest-ranking non-commissioned officer, an E8, was called Top. They liked him too. With the grunts it was as if nobody wanted to know them by their real names. Or maybe because their real names never rang a bell as to what made them different from all the others. But nicknames did. The kid from Indiana was Indy; the kid from Florida was Gator; the fellow who looked like him was Elvis; the boy who always got them from home was called Oreo; the tough guy from the Bronx who always kept to himself was called Loner; and almost every outfit had a Tex.

For a long time with him being a new recruit he was just called, "Shorty." But in Nam they started calling him "Rat" and he didn't know why. He would soon find out why. But it was after an incident in which a lot of them could have been killed that they switched to the more affectionate nickname for him. He liked that because nobody was killed and everybody liked him being that nickname. Here's how it came about:

For a while there was a lull in activities at their base. He had spent a couple days writing letters and going around to the other platoons and meeting new guys. By the fourth day his buddy Indy came up with an idea to break the monotony. He said he had to get rid of some mortar rounds because a new supply was coming in. He asked if he wanted to fire off a few with him.

Of course he would. Indy explained how he calculated trajectory and the kind of stuff that was Greek to him. Then he watched his buddy send off six rounds. They heard the distant explosions. When it came his turn, he took his time. It was like bottle rockets and the Fourth of July back home. He sent three down the chute. *Whump, whump, whump.* But the fourth one went straight up in the air and sort of hovered there …. He yelled, "*SHORT ROUND!*" Everyone dived for cover. It came right down on them!

It would have killed them all but luckily it was a dud. From that day on he had his nickname. They called him, "*Short Round.*"

In the days that followed, everyone seemed to go out of their way calling him that. He just grinned and felt good about it. For once this nickname gave him a warm and fuzzy feeling. He knew they accepted him now. And it was a heck of a lot better than them calling him, "*Hey you.*"

Not long after that he was to go on to fame and glory as the platoon's fearless one and only peerless Tunnel Rat, or so his buddies said proudly. That came about the same way as his curiosity over what it was like to be a Point Man. He had asked to try it with their own Point Man, Loner, and it so surprised the usually quiet fellow that he took this crazy new recruit under his wing and taught him everything he knew about staying alive and doing it right. That was important because a lot of guys behind him bet their lives on him doing it right.

When Loner went home, Short Round got the job with everyone's blessing and did great at it. It was the kind of job that paid big dividends if you didn't screw up and missed spotting a hidden booby trap before the men stumbled into the blast zone. If that happened, the Point Man and everyone up front paid the price for him not spotting and disarming it. But Loner had trained him well. Short Round had the eyes of a hawk and the natural instincts to be careful.

When they came into an area of underground tunnels, curiosity hit him again. It was the same curiosity that could just as easily get him killed.

On patrol they had come upon two Vietnamese ladies in a panic. Their Kit Carson Scout [native guide and translator] talked to them to find out what was wrong.

Apparently two little girls, who often played in one of the village tunnels for about an hour each day, had not come back. They had been gone for almost three hours now. The old ladies were afraid something had happened to them; that maybe they had been kidnapped.

When Top asked for volunteers to go down into that tunnel and look for the little girls, Short Round held up his hand. Not only was he interested but his size made him a natural candidate for the job, much to everyone else's relief.

But everyone in the platoon was against him going because they sure didn't want to lose their very valuable Point Man. But Short Round wanted to know what those tunnels were like underground so it was with this curiosity that he told Top that he would go and check it out.

The two worried women led him to a place in the jungle; then pointed down. He looked around and he couldn't see what they were talking about until they touched a cover that had foliage on it. When they lifted it off he saw a framed opening leading downward. That's when he had to strip for action. The Top took his pack and rifle away from him and asked for his dog tags just in case something happened to him while he was down there. At least they had his tags for identification. The Top handed him his .45 so that was what he went with, his flashlight in one hand and the Top's heavy . 45 in the other.

Looking very carefully at his surroundings, Short Round crawled through the small opening headfirst because the shaft was too tight to turn around in the tunnel. It was a few degrees cooler but the humidity was something else.

He lit his light at once because he didn't want to trigger any booby trap. A short ways down the tunnel turned at a right angle; angled downward and gradually became much wider and taller as it opened up to where he could almost stand up. He moved along slowly and carefully. In the distance he thought he heard girlish giggling and laughter. Then he saw them. They had a lantern with them.

Short Round turned off his flashlight so he wouldn't scare them. As he came up on the two little girls he saw them sitting in the dirt happily playing. When they spotted him they screamed in panic. But he kept his voice calm and called to them. After awhile when they saw he was not going to harm them, they slowly came up to him. He gave each of them a hug and pointed them to the way out of the tunnel. They went and when they crawled out of the opening above ground the two little old ladies let them have it.

Apparently they had just forgotten about the time.

When Top and the rest of the guys praised him, Short Round felt good. Grinning broadly, Top gave him back his gear. As Short Round returned the NCO's heavy handgun, Top just grinned and said, "Your .45 and holster will be on the next supply chopper."

Late that afternoon they brought him his own new U.S. Colt .45 and he spent the next couple hours in his hooch cleaning his rifle; then he practiced dismantling the .45 and putting it back together again with his eyes closed. Short Round suspected that he would be asked to volunteer again soon.

2

How the Enemy
Hid Underfoot

During the early phases of the Vietnam War it became apparent that we were facing guerilla warfare. We just were not aware of how extensive it was and what an almost insurmountable problem it would be. In 1966, sudden explosive contacts with the North Vietnamese Army often ended with comments like this one from a young Marine: "The Commies were so close we could hear them breathing. By dawn however, the enemy was gone." Or, after a good-sized force of NVA was spotted by a recon team and artillery fire was called down on them, more VC flooded down on the team. A reaction platoon was rushed to help the recon Marines but by the time it arrived on the scene, the large number of enemy had somehow disappeared. During one six-day period, infantry companies fanned out looking for the enemy in the jungle and found them nearly everywhere. The encounters were always brief and violent but before artillery could be brought to bear, the enemy as usual somehow slipped through their fingers. In another instance, Marines had just finished clearing a village when VC suddenly popped up from huts they had just found to be empty! The Marines swiftly engaged them in a short but deadly clash before the enemy once again disappeared into the scenery like ghosts.

No one really realized how complicated the enemy's magic disappearing act was until years after the war. Only then did we understand the full extent of their tactics. Only then did the surviving tacticians behind it all gradually reveal how they carried on an undercover war right under our feet. Even today, decades after that terrible time, what they accomplished underground is incredible, even to describe. But they did it. Here's how it all started:

In his book *Viet Cong and NVA Tunnels and Fortifications of the Vietnam War* (Fortress) by Gordon L. Rottman, the author said that the tunnel systems were begun in the late 1940s and evolved through the first Indochina War with France. "They were first used to hide wanted individuals, then families as the fighting worsened, and to hide supplies; before long, whole villages and guerrilla units were hiding in them. They were well developed by the time Americans arrived in 1965 and continued to expand as the war progressed. While tunnel building was popular in the late 1940s, it really got going between 1948 and 1949 during the Indochina War. The reason it was so popular then was because it was a symbol of solidarity between villages that were intent on evading France's sweeps through these areas. During this time, almost every Vietnamese family had a secret underground room where they could hide a Viet Minh soldier. Of course once these secret hiding places were discovered the soldier could be caught or killed. So the Vietnamese realized the need for a more complex tunnel system that linked to other similar systems. So, during the Vietnam War this system was vigorously upgraded. As tunnel building shifted into high gear, the communists even published a ten-page how-to-do-it tunnel-making guide that detailed every bit of it. The people eagerly embraced the idea.

During the day the peasants worked the fields but at night, under the cover of darkness, they continued with their underground excavating activities. Each village dug their own separate tunnels. For security sake no village knew where another village had made its tunnels. Some led to rivers but others actually went under the river. Many involved a water trap. Today's cave divers call them sumps, a pool of water that collects in a low place. But that pool of water in a tunnel or cave may be more than just a pool of water. In 1932, French speleologist Norbert Casteret was exploring a cave in Montespan, France when he was stopped by a similar pool of water. He wondered if it was just a water block to the same tunnel that continued beyond it. With candle and matches wrapped in a rubber bathing cap he stripped and waded into the pool. When he came to its back wall he dived down and swam through the darkness and came up in a cave that had not seen mankind for the last 20,000 years! Surrounding him were clay images of animals worshiped by Ice Age Man. It was the find of the century.

Similarly these Vietnam pools of water at the end of a tunnel were often constructed to stop any pursuers. If you waded into it and ducked underwater to clear the overhead you emerged in the same continuing dry tunnel. Hidden trap doors under heavy baskets of stored rice also were used to access tunnels a level below the one you were in.

As directed by the Viet Cong's tunnel guidebook, the tunnels were made in a specific way. Builders were told to purposely design the top level of communication tunnels in a zigzag fashion. Not undulating but sharp zigzags which made it harder for the enemy to explore them and easier for the VC to hide and ambush any intruders. Zigzags also helped protect against explosive charges. Whatever soil was excavated at night was dumped into bomb craters or river systems.

Just the thought that with the most primitive of tools villagers could dig these areas underground is in itself unbelievable. Think of all the roots they would encounter in their jungle settings, think of the problems of ventilation and the dangers of cave-ins. How would anyone with just shovels and scoops manage such a seemingly dangerous project?

Thanks to the sand and rocks of America's West, most of our miners' tunnels had to use the post and lintel kind of tunnel construction. Not so in Vietnam. Their soil was made for tunnel digging. It is a laterite clay, rich in iron and aluminum that makes it a super tunneling material; one that not only supports the tunnel shape but in the dry season the underground structures turned as hard as a brick and became almost impermeable.

The tunnels were oftentimes directly under the feet of the military people above. It gave the enemy an opportunity to pop out of a tunnel to seize weapons, grab food stocks, and to attack right in the center of our bases and to keep on fighting from different areas. As mentioned the upper level tunnels were zigzagged purposely because when the enemy detected the tunnel they often first tossed in grenades or a Bangalore – several connected explosives – and the zigzag features largely blocked those blasts.

The way diggers began these tunnels was unique. Usually a narrow hole was dug straight down to a depth of 9 to 15 feet. One of the diggers waited at the top of this hole with a basket tied to a long rope. The digger in the hole would shovel earth into the basket, which was then hauled to the surface. At the same time, 30 feet away, another hole was begun and went down to the same depth. Then the tunnel diggers would make a right angle turn and start digging toward each other. By shouting back and forth at the end of these tunnels the diggers dug until they met in the middle. This was repeated over and over as the tunnel lengthened. Later those vertical shafts were either filled in or used as entry and exit holes hidden beneath cleverly camouflaged covers.

The diggers never tunneled upward, always downward so they could dispose of the earth. Because of the torrential rains that occurred especially during the monsoon season they always allowed for a downward gradient in their communication tunnels so that the water would drain into wells underground. The entire operation was shared by all the villagers, with different jobs for everyone. The elder men made the baskets for carrying the soil, while the elder women cooked. Young men and women used their strength to dig the earth with shovels and scoops. Even the children helped out by gathering leaves that would be used for camouflaging the trap doors on the surface. The most popular digging gear was worn-out spades and hoes. In the beginning the tunnels were one-room affairs that would hide a single soldier, but then they enlarged them so they would hide an entire family. In each village each family had a responsibility for its part of the tunnel. After that, various huts in the village were joined by tunnels. That tunnel was then linked to meet those of nearby villages. Finally, this underground network contained main communication tunnels, secret tunnels, false tunnels; they even had signs along the way telling strangers which direction to go and who they were. Each village had guides that were available to take people from one district to another before handing them over to another guide, all of this was going on underground. In time, everything expanded until there were not only sleeping rooms, sniping hides called spider holes with cleverly camouflaged lids to conceal them, there were also air raid shelters, latrines, hospitals, kitchens, large rooms for political meetings; others that were huge store rooms for food and armaments; even chambers where they could keep water buffalo.

Other underground compartments were workshops where they could produce homemade bombs and booby traps. Some even acted as primitive forges for making anti-personal mines. The gigantic storage areas contained baskets of rice, the single most important food product to sustain this underground community.

There were even temporary graveyards. Those Vietnamese who were heavily involved in developing this underground community described underground chambers that were capable of concealing a complete 105-mm Field Artillery Howitzer where they were kept stripped and oiled ready for reassembling for action. Above ground, tanks rumbled and thrashed about; the bombs and artillery shells left their marks and foot-soldiers moved through the jungle foliage, completely unaware that the enemy was often directly beneath them, about 12 feet down, carrying on a far-reaching hidden hive of activity.

Certainly all such things required ventilation. They had nothing mechanical, no electricity to run them. Everything had to be done by hand. Through the entire tunnel system cleverly hidden lengths of bamboo served as their ventilating systems, even down to a depth of three tunnel tiers. They were all put in the ground obliquely so they were less likely to flood the caverns below with rainwater. Great care was taken to make sure that they were cleverly camouflaged on the surface.

Cooking was done by little old ladies on what they called the Dien Bien Phu kitchen stove. These were constructed in such a way as to be as smokeless as possible. Originally designed to be used underground during the war with the French, they were further refined in the 1960s during the war with the Americans. When a fire was started in the stove the smoke was directed by ducts to escape from several surface ground level chimneys. The diluted smoke was thus never detected by aerial surveillance. The system worked well but there were enough leaks in it to make it quite uncomfortable for the women cooks.

According to one Vietnam Major, tunnel life was not pleasant, "The tunnels we were in stank and we stank. They were usually very hot and we were always sweating." He went on to say that they carried with them their daily ration of food comprised of a snowball-sized ball of cooked rice and dried fish. "We hid during the day but at night we tried to cook the rice for eating the next day. If there was no time to prepare the rice we went without food for the whole day until the next night when we tried to come up. It really wasn't possible for us to cook underground, the smoke was always asphyxiating. We just could not breathe." He continued to say that sometimes they were driven to attack the Americans just to make them go away so they could come up to the surface at night and cook in the open. He said, "You can't imagine what kind of pleasure that was."

A Vietnamese medical officer during the war agreed with him saying that usually the cooking was very unpleasant underground and that often rather than cook they stuck with dry food. He added that it was impossible to cook up on the surface because the smoke would attract too much attention. Ironically, the more Americans there were above them helped resolve some of the VC's food problems. He said that the soldiers' canned food rations were always left around after infantry attacks. It included such delicacies as canned meat, fried rice; noodles with prawns; cigarettes and chocolate. Apparently the hungry subterraneans swiftly scarfed up those leavings with gusto.

Also, when they grew short of food they came to the surface and grew such things as sweet potatoes, bananas, cassava and manioc. He said the Americans were very clever and were aware of the fact that when they saw these plants growing in an area together they were close to where a secret tunnel entrance would be found. But even though the underground inhabitants knew it was dangerous to grow these plants near their tunnels it was just as dangerous to starve to death.

In the end, however, the one food source they could always count on and the one they enjoyed the most were tunnel rats. They were always plentiful and according to one of these underground inhabitants, "They were delicious and provided plenty of protein. I found grilled rat had a better flavor than chicken or duck."

One of the questions that would first come to mind for anyone planning to spend any time living underground was what would you do about light?

Most of the normal lighting used by these people came from oil lamps, especially those that they made out of old American shell casings with a simple wick that coiled down into the nut oil that these lamps burned. A somewhat larger model and very popular lamp was made simply from a small brown medicine bottle with a nut wedged into its mouth and a wick that protruded through a hole drilled through the nut. To keep these from being knocked over easily they all had a piece of scrape metal attached to their bottom as a weight.

Some of these tunnel inhabitants who spent five years or more of the war living underground had a difficult time living in daylight after the war above ground. Their eyes had so adapted to the dark that normal daylight traumatized them. Not to mention the trauma of continual life or death circumstances they lived under most of the time they were underground. None of them ever knew when a direct hit from a bomb would cave in their world permanently or if their sleeping quarters were deep enough to keep the war from crashing in on them. One Vietnamese soldier who did survive the war described these fears as documented by author Rottman in his book:

"My own personal possessions for nearly five years were just those I could fit inside a shoulder bag. I had a big American army belt to which was attached an American water bottle [canteen]. I had a nylon roof sheet made from parachutes two and a half meters long which where possible was pegged to the roof to prevent earth falling all over me especially during American bombing operations. I had a nylon waterproof cape during the rainy season, a hammock, a lamp made out of an old menthol bottle, a dagger, a rifle and a rice bag. The heaviest thing I had was the rice bag which weighed 10 kilograms [22 ½-pounds] The main problems which never left us were malnutrition and malaria."

Such was life among the human moles who found that during the war they were safer there that above ground where life was completely uncertain for them.

3

Something Awaits
In the Darkness Below

Some weeks after finding the little girls, Short Round's outfit was camped beside a village where there once were a lot of huts clustered together. Believing it to be a Viet Cong hangout, fighter-bombers were ordered to drop napalm on it and everyone was burned up and frozen in place. It reminded Short Round of a *National Geographic* magazine article with pictures of what remained of the people of Pompeii after the volcano wiped them out. Caught in whatever position they were in when the hot ash settled on them, they were frozen in time in solidified lava.

One old villager told them that there were still Viet Cong in the area and that they were underground in a series of tunnels that started in one of the hooches. Nobody wanted to go exploring in them. The officers left it entirely up to any volunteers willing to go. Since Short Round was still curious about what he might find there, he volunteered to go again despite his buddies trying to dissuade him, reminding him that he had a pregnant wife and a son back home. But he was determined to do it anyway.

He looked at the Old Man who was looking at the ground and confidently spoke up, "Yeah, oh yeah, I'll do it."

Again, as he had done many times before, Indy slapped him up side his helmet. Short Round didn't blame him really. He was trying to knock some sense into his head. "After all," he thought to himself, "there's a fine line between bravery and stupidity and I keep crossing it."

No Point Man now, he had switched hats. He was a rat once more …. The Old Man showed him several tunnel openings and told him to pick one. Short Round randomly pointed at the closest one to him. As his buddies held his rifle, backpack and dog tags he armed himself with his .45 in one hand and flashlight in the other.

When he turned around he noticed that half the company was staring at him in a very solemn way. Almost as if they thought this was the last time they would ever see him again. All the while they were telling him to be careful and wishing him good luck. So down he went.

He entered the black hole on his belly and after only a dozen feet of crawling, the passageway widened. He was surprised to find that he was almost able to stand up. He marveled at the size of it and figured it must have taken people years to dig the thing. Abruptly it looked like he was coming to the end of it. He was disappointed as his flashlight illuminated the apparent dead end. He started to turn around and head back when he heard someone. It sounded as though they were singing. That didn't make any sense to him at all. The singing sounded spooky and far off. So he turned back into the tunnel again.

He went in the direction of the sound trying to reach the voice. What he found was that the tunnel had not dead-ended at all. The tunnel made a sharp turn to the left. It was easily overlooked. He figured it was made purposely that way to throw off any enemy who might be exploring it.

When he saw a flash of lantern light and a shadow, Short Round instantly turned off his flashlight. The man had his back to him. Short Round quietly slipped up closer and closer to him. Finally he was literally just a foot away from the man when he turned and saw him.

Instinctively the man grabbed for his wrist. As he did Short Round fired twice and dropped him in his tracks.

Immediately he was aware of one major drawback of this tunnel hunting operation. He couldn't hear anything except his ears roaring from the explosion. He felt as if he had suddenly stuck his head underwater. All sound had been snuffed out except for the tremendous roar in his ears.

Short Round sagged down beside the lifeless body while his hammering heart slowly came down to regular. In the days before he had become a soldier doing something like this would have been unthinkable to him. But now that he was a soldier he really felt no sorrow. This was the enemy and he was sworn to kill him. One less of the enemy was one less chance that another soldier would be killed by this man.

Since all of his fellow soldiers were family to him this was one family he would protect at all costs.

When he finally felt up to it again he decided that his job in the tunnel was over. He took the man's AK-47 so he could show his buddies why they had heard his gunshot.

After he crawled back the way he had come and came out, his buddies swarmed around him throwing questions at him so fast that he couldn't hear what they were saying. Mainly because his hearing was still out of whack. Everything seemed to come to him as muffled echoes. Indy, his buddy, was bear-hugging him and slapping his helmet like mad.

When he was finally able to hear something again he heard Top say, "Short Round, you are one crazy little guy!"

What with everything he had experienced, that pumped him up pretty good. It had scared the dickens out of him but he liked that feeling. The feeling of being on edge. He liked it so much he knew that he had to do it again.

Abruptly he realized he was ravenously hungry and so he wolfed down his C rations. Then he was ready to go again.

4

Their Incredible Underground World

Not many tunnel rats ever explored further than the first line of tunnels close to the surface. Mainly because the trap doors leading to tunnels below that one were so cleverly concealed that they were seldom discovered by the tunnel rat. After the war however, Americans found just how extensive these underground passageways actually were. There were hundreds of miles of them!

One intrepid tunnel explorer was Jan Shrader who was attached to the military command in Vietnam after the war. Shrader was amazed when he explored one of the second level sections near Saigon and found chambers at that level that measured fifteen feet high. He said, "It was incredible, with all that space, what they kept there or what was done in there I can't imagine … the thing we found more than anything else was arms and munitions in perfect condition of storage. For example, there was artillery ammunition for 57-mm recoilless rifles; each round was in an individually handmade little tin can with a sweated lead joint and cap, also laboriously handmade. Each rifle we found was wrapped in rags and Cosmoline [a brown waxy rust inhibitor used by the military to preserve weapons] and very nicely done up with a little metal tag tied with a little piece of wire. You wouldn't want to write anything on paper because that wouldn't last very long in the tunnels, and they knew that because they had been doing it so damn long. So they had little pieces of soft metal that they wrote on with a stylus in their own symbols, for what was wrapped up in that package."

But that was not all that Shrader found. He discovered workshop areas in the tunnels whose main reason for being was to copy armaments and to actually make small arms, Chinese copies of Thompson sub-machine guns and other French designs. They would take a French machine gun, which they had captured from the French and in that tunnel workshop they would begin turning out copies of it that were made by hand. They also made ammunition, hand grenades, and lots of mines.

At the end of 1969 a company was busily blowing up bunkers they found in the woods northwest of Cu Chi when one of their sergeants saw what appeared to be an air vent into a tunnel. But they were unable to find the entrance to it no matter how hard they searched. So they decided to dig down the air vent until they broke through into the tunnel. As they dug down, they came across wood blocking their way. They sawed through it. Then, surprisingly they hit concrete. This really baffled them for a while. They figured whatever was in that tunnel was being protected extra heavily from aerial bombardment. So they hammered away at the concrete until they smashed a hole through, then none of them believed their eyes at what they saw.

There was enough equipment in that underground room to print an entire newspaper, and that included a fifteen hundred pound printing press in perfect working condition with rows upon rows of type – 37 trays of type stacked along the walls of this huge six foot high, 30 by 40 foot chamber with a table-full of ink and dyes in 5-gallon cans and thousands of pamphlets – two tons in all of propaganda publications that had been printed there during the war!

Other American military searching these complex subterranean passageways after the war discovered enormous underground storerooms. These too were fifteen feet high where the underground workers were hiding parts of large artillery pieces. These would be disassembled on the surface, carried down into the tunnels piece-by-piece and stored. Later, the enemy intended bringing the pieces to the surface where the artillery could be reassembled and ready for use.

One military official was quoted as saying, "No wonder we never found their guns outside. In one set of underground chambers we found two 105-mm field guns. These two 105s were over forty years old and they were still in perfect condition. Can you imagine it, he said, imagine putting those great field howitzers to bed every night in a tunnel," he said. "One reason our casualties ran so high, was because you could never figure where Charlie got his weapons, his rocket launchers, and big pieces, fired them, then hid them, then fired them again. It was hard work for him to do it, but it was a damn lot harder for us to figure it out. The first time we found this stuff deep inside a tunnel we couldn't believe it."

As astonishing as these discoveries were, it was a fact that in 1966 the Viet Cong managed to steal an entire tank from the ARVN (Army of the Republic of Vietnam, also known as The South Vietnamese Army), which was a stunning event that brought on all kinds of government consternation. No one could understand how this M-48 tank simply disappeared from this ARVN unit. But three years later the Americans found it again – in a tunnel! It had been buried – entirely covered up – and tunnels had been dug around it.

This huge metal monster was being used by the VC as an underground armored command center. When found everything still worked! The batteries, the lights, even the radio were all working!

At the end of November 1966 the military intelligence for ARVN detailed the results of their interrogation of a captured Viet Cong platoon leader who reported to have been ordered to switch on a generator for re-charging the batteries for a large signals unit in a forest. This unit was found deep underground where the VC working with it were using it for intercepting radio transmissions, tapping telephones and breaking codes. Their members were fluent in many languages. It was a signals intelligence unit and a similar one was found by our infantry in use by the North Vietnamese that had it hidden underground as well. What was learned from all this was that all of our radio communications from the 1st and 25th Divisions had been logged and translated into Vietnamese so that the enemy knew in advance our every move!

During the war, one sharp-eyed officer noticed that the bamboo in one area looked odd, as though it had been bundled up and planted there on purpose. It looked too tall and too neat to be natural. So when he had his men start poking around, one of the first things they uncovered was the entrance to a large tunnel complex. When they blew this up, it was as if though they had kicked the top off of an anthill. It immediately uncovered entrances to many other tunnels. As they checked them out they found that they had uncovered an underground munitions workshop. They found many underground bunkers with bamboo roofs and strings of communication tunnels in which they found drill presses, little forges, a bellows system using charcoal, a complete workshop; piles of scrap metal to be melted down into pots for new shell casings that were made with sand moulds. Their homemade grenades had wood handles on them and small firing chains. Ancient drill presses in upright models were hand-cranked. They all worked.

In author Rottman's *Viet Cong and NVA Tunnels and Fortifications of the Vietnam War*, he quotes one of the workers who described what life was like in this underground printing operation:

> "It was a dreadful existence. One lived by the hour; one was alive one hour and might be killed the next. A person could be sitting and talking to you and be dead within five minutes. With the sheer quantity of ammunition the Americans used there were times when survival was just a lottery. The tunnels were the safest thing we had, but they were not impregnable. Personally I

had a small shelter in which I slept. It was 80-cm by 78-cm and one meter high [31.5 inches long by 27.5 inches wide and three feet high.] You can imagine what it was like for a man in that hole, night after night. I had not dug the shelter too deep for we learned from bitter experience that the deeper the shelter, the greater the chance of being buried alive after a bombing attack, so I built a moderately strong shelter that could deal with the bomb fragments. When the enemy carried out their anti-guerilla operations above, I went into my sleeping shelter, lit a candle and read books or wrote poems until the air was so foul I had to extinguish the candle and lie in the eternal night, listening to the tanks and guns above me. I did not know, nor did my comrades, whether we had judged the depth of our tunnels correctly. One lay there, wondering if a tank would crush through the ceiling of your sleeping chamber and crush you to death or worse, not quite to death."

5

Always Another Underground Surprise

After Short Round's initial good luck taking out the VC in his last tunnel operation, the Old Man pointed to the anthill of openings they recently uncovered and asked him to take his pick. It made no difference to him. He pointed at another one that had a larger opening. As he dropped down into it he realized it was a much bigger tunnel. He hadn't gone 20 feet when he was actually able to stand up inside it.

To keep himself from being discovered by whoever might be in the tunnel he shined his flashlight only for a count of three before he turned it off. Then as he progressed in the darkness he counted to 30. Then he turned it on again to get his bearings and in three seconds he went back to crawling through the dark for the next 30 seconds.

Suddenly in the distance he saw the glow of lantern light. He thought to himself, "Oh, oh, here we go again!"

The light glow was about a hundred feet in front of him so he kept his flashlight turned off as he inched closer to the distant light.

As he drew closer he could hear the sound of voices. Once he reached a point where the sounds seemed to be coming from, he realized there was a large hole in the floor of the tunnel. And he saw the top of a bamboo ladder that led straight down into a much larger underground room. It was a gigantic pit that had been dug down there. That's where the glow of light came from. Carefully and quietly he inched toward the opening and looked over the edge of it.

Some distance from the hole he saw two men in the lantern light smoking. He recognized from the sweet odor that it was marijuana.

The large room was filled with things. One corner had a stack of AK-47s along with many cases of ammunition. Not far from that he saw bandages and all kinds of hospital supplies. Then there were maps and piles of documents. Beyond them, many barrels full of rice extended far into the cavern, enough to feed an army. What he was looking at was an underground supply room that had everything in it from guns, food, bandages along with stacks of maps and documents that would be of interest to our intelligence people.

The question now was what he should do about it. The VC down there seemed to be set for a long time, talking and puffing away on their weed. Short Round surely wasn't going to go down that ladder and try to take them prisoner. The instant he made his presence known he knew he would be dead.

But he stayed there near the hole, sweating profusely and wondering if his buddies outside would think, after so long a time, that something had happened to him.

He sat there for fifteen minutes trying to decide what to do when all of a sudden one of the VC turned and came toward the ladder. The other one was right behind him.

Short Round crouched down in the darkness near the hole because he now knew what he had to do if they started up the ladder.

He stayed low in the darkness with his .45 ready for them as he heard them climbing the bamboo ladder.

Once the first VC put his hands on the ledge and started to climb onto it, Short Round fired. As the man fell backwards Short Round jumped to the opening and fired at the other man, but the round only creased his head. Short Round quickly fired twice more and that did it.

As the smoke cleared he turned on his flashlight and looked down into the pit at their lifeless bodies. He was shaking all over.

Finally, he made himself slowly climb down the ladder and step over the bodies. He realized then that he had that underwater feeling again of being stuffed up and unable to hear anything but the roar in his head. Also, he had hurt his hand on his helmet from the gun's recoil because he was unable to lock his elbow when he fired at the second man.

Despite his pain and deafness he looked around the huge cavern in awe. He had never seen so many weapons or so many barrels of rice. Enough food and supplies to last the enemy a long time. Maps and documents were there too.

Out of a crazy notion about how much rice there was, he ran his arms down into a wooden barrel of it and was surprised to feel paper deep down inside it. He pulled out some of them and figured they were very important for someone to have hidden them in the rice. Short Round moved around picking up things that looked important like documents and maps. The papers were all written in a language he couldn't understand but he knew that they could be translated. He grabbed everything that looked important and took them with him as he moved back through the passageway and came to the surface.

The looks on the faces of his buddies was one of shocked surprise because they thought for sure that this time, Short Round had gone down for the count. When the company commander rushed up to greet him he even had tears in his eyes! Short Round couldn't believe they all felt that way about him. It made him feel like a giant. His commander said that they heard four shots fired and thought for sure that was the end of him. They were just trying to figure out who was going to go in and recover his remains when he popped out. Everybody was sure relieved to see him back again.

He told them what he had seen and what he had to do to

the two VC that were there. They immediately brought a Kit Carson Scout up to see what the documents were that he had saved. The Vietnamese translator said that they were different times and destinations for attacks that they planned to make. The commander was beaming all over. He said, "Short Round I'm making you an E4 plus whatever award I can see fitting."

"Great!" shouted the short soldier. "My wife's going to appreciate that pay raise!" He couldn't be happier. But he realized that wasn't the end of it because the captain wanted them to go back and blow up all that rice.

Short Round argued that he didn't have any experience handling high explosives but the officer said he would send an expert with him to show him what to do.

They got on the radio and ordered four bricks of C4, which would come in with the next chopper. Later that day they picked it up, along with blasting caps and detonator.

Once Short Round and the explosive's expert placed it all around in the pit area and got out of there, they detonated the whole works.

As the company moved off some 300 yards from the village where they had found all the tunnels, the Air Force jets came over and bombed everything to oblivion. Short Round said that when they left, the place looked like an empty parking lot.

6

A Special Kind of Bravery

Here are two personal descriptions by experienced tunnel rats as to what it was like crawling down into those dark, extremely dangerous places. This is from *Tunnel Rats* by Sandy MacGregor and Jimmy Thomson. What follows is a description of what it was like to be a Tunnel Rat from an Australian solder's view:

"You launch yourself head first down a hole in the ground that's scarcely wide enough for your shoulders. After a couple of meters of sliding and wriggling straight down, the narrow tunnel takes a U-turn toward the surface, then twists again before heading off further than you can see with the battery-powered lamp attached to your cap.

Because the tunnel has recently been full of smoke and tear-gas, you are wearing a gas mask. The eyepieces steam up and the sound of your own breathing competes with the thump of your heart to deafen you. You know you are not safe. You are in your enemy's domain and one of your comrades – a friend – has already died in a hole in the ground just like this one.

This is the stuff of nightmares: a tunnel that is almost too small to crawl along, dug by and for slightly built and wiry Vietnamese, not broad-backed Aussies or Americans.

Every inch forward has to be checked for bobby traps, so you have a bayonet in one hand. Every corner could conceal an enemy soldier, perhaps one that can retreat no further, so you have a pistol in the other. There is no room to turn around. Going forward is difficult enough; backing out is neigh impossible. You know that the enemy knows you are there. You know your miner's light makes a perfect target. You switch it off.

The silence is ominous, though not as complete as your heart throbs through your body. The velvet darkness is all-engulfing.

Then it begins to close in on you and you begin to lose your breath. You become light-headed, then dizzy, then confused as the air runs out. Reason and sense evaporate as the darkness claims you. But you get a grip … you breathe … you bring it all back under control because the alternative – blind panic – means death. And you move on.

That's how it felt to be a capital Tunnel Rat. That's what it was like to know real fear – fear of being trapped, fear of an unseen enemy, fear of ever-present booby traps and most of all fear of the unknown. There was no military text book, training class, or official orders that told the diggers in three field-troop who went down the Vietcong's tunnels what to expect and how to deal with it, for the simple read on that they were the first. No Australian or American had ever explored a major tunnel system before."

From: *The Tunnels of Cu Chi: A Harrowing Account of America's Tunnel Rats in the Underground Battlefields of Vietnam,* author Tom Mangold and John Penycate wrote:

"At the height of the Vietnam conflict, a complex system of secret underground tunnels sprawled from Cu Chi Province to the edge of Saigon. In those, the Viet Cong cached their weapons, tended their wounded, and prepared to strike. They had only one enemy; U.S. soldiers small and wiry enough to be able to maneuver through the guerilla's narrow domain."

The authors include both sides of life in the underground tunnels from the Vietnamese to the American tunnel rats. Here are comments from the enemy's point of view:

"Before I go, I'd like to talk to the guy who controls those incredible men in the tunnels." That man was Lieutenant Nguyen Thanh Linh. "Those tunnels were everything to us in Crimp," he explained nearly two decades after Lieutenant Colonel Eyster's grudging words of admiration. "There were no set battles, but everyone who could fire a rifle did so. We used them for constant surprise sniper attacks and we used them, most importantly, for observation. Thanks to the tunnels, we could remain with the Americans, see how their troops behaved and reacted, watch their mistakes. Our observations helped us decide what kinds of booby traps to set and where to set them. "You know, we even saw helicopters bringing special water for the Americans to wash themselves, and we realized the soldiers used nothing Vietnamese. I had been ordered by my superiors to provide intelligence about American battlefield tactics, and the tunnels made all of this possible."

The enemy occasionally used their tunnels to draw the Americans into their traps. They soon learned our habits. For instance they knew that only a few of our smallest soldiers would be able to enter the tunnels and come looking for them, while the rest of the soldiers hung around the entrance waiting for the rat to reappear. So here's what they sometimes did: The VC, inside the tunnel, which they had set up as a trap for the Americans, would wait for the tunnel rat to appear. The usual six-foot vertical entrance turned at right angles at its bottom as the tunnel angled downward. As soon as the rat came down, either head first or feet first, the waiting enemy either bayoneted or shot him. Immediately there was commotion topside as his buddies flocked around the opening trying to retrieve his body. The VC then went deeper in his tunnel to a remote control he had stashed there. He triggered it and a captured claymore mine cleverly concealed above ground in a bush near the entrance peppered everyone with a blast of 400 lethal ball bearings.

Topside survivors would then blow up the tunnel with grenades or explosive charges while the enemy was long gone through a series of trap doors into other tunnels that might take him miles away. One Vietnamese even described how he would escape through a trap door hidden in the roof of a tunnel, then on the other side he would drag a huge hamper of rice onto the trap door, climb atop it and when he triggered the explosion the concussion would lift him, the rice and the trapdoor several inches in the air.

Even the Landing Zones often cleared to bring in

choppers of troops were not overlooked from this devilish plotting. Concealed claymores in the surrounding treetops were set to trigger automatically from the downdraft of the rotors. Chopper and men took the brunt of it.

Putting aside the many different booby traps the enemy left for us in their deadly holes, these underground tunnels were a breeding ground for all manner of biting organisms that fed on those who went there. The job or task of being a tunnel rat called for a special kind of bravery. It took a special temperament and courage because these men, who crawled down into these mysterious black holes, were required to perform the most stressful tasks imaginable. They were required to crawl through pitch-black, narrow earthen tunnels that were often tight, hot, stinking and deadly dangerous. They faced the threat of death at any moment. All of those in combat knew that the reason the enemy could suddenly disappear after a fast and furious engagement above ground, was that they had suddenly disappeared down one of their many underground passageways. There they remained, heavily armed, biding their time until night fell; then like vampires they quietly crawled out to create their deadly mischief.

So not only was that danger constantly awaiting them, but if the tunnel rat had any experience at all, he knew that there might also be booby traps that could be set off merely by touching a concealed wire in the darkness as they fumbled their way along; or perhaps in the darkness sat one or more of the armed enemy just waiting for them.

While they are a little afraid of turning on a hand light for fear it might make them an instant target, not lighting that light was also a hazard. In the dark they could bump into all kinds of trouble, not to mention enemies of another kind.

In the tunnels with them was a welcoming committee of fire ants, scorpions, poisonous centipedes, fleas, real rats, and sometimes a few sullen snakes like the three-step. About the size of a fat green shoelace this viper was so-named because once he bit you by your third step you dropped down dead. In truth, you could probably get in a lot more steps before the Grim Reaper got you. But the bottom line was usually the same: a bite from this unfriendly fellow was generally fatal. Not the kind of welcoming committee you wanted to meet in the dark, but certainly the kind the VC sometimes left behind in numbers tied to dangling vines twisting sinuously and silently in the dark, watching you.

The largest complex of tunnels at Cu Chi occurred in the Saigon area about 40 or 50 kilometers from the center of Vietnam's largest city. In Tom Mangold's *The Tunnels of Cu Chi* book he quotes a Vietnamese official explaining that, "We used (the tunnels) for constant surprise sniper attacks, and we used them, most importantly, for observation. Thanks to the tunnels, we could remain with the Americans; see how their troops behaved and reacted; watch their mistakes. Our observations helped us decide what kind of booby traps to set and where to set them."

In April 1966 a lieutenant and an SP4 from his platoon were investigating an underground tunnel north of Cu Chi when they found a suspicious looking feature that made them curious as to what might be hidden behind it. The tunnel wall looked strange. It was camouflaged to look like a tunnel wall but this one was made out of hardboard. It took them two hours to hack through it with their bayonets. Behind it they found a heavy two-foot long worn wooden box with Chinese characters printed on it.

They dragged it out into the open and speculated what was in it. Nothing would have surprised them more at what they found. As they pried the lid off they were stunned to find the box filled with gold bars!

For a while they just leaned back and stared at it with open mouths. They had found a King's Ransom! Each bar was about five inches long and one and a half inches thick. The two men were so shocked by their sudden good fortune, they didn't know what to do. They were both now richer than they had ever dreamed. Their minds raced over the possibilities. They talked excitedly about how best to keep the treasure they had found. First, they thought they should leave it there and come back for it after the war. But realized that was too chancy and someone else could find it. Then they thought maybe they could share it with their platoon without anyone else finding out about it. But that was crazy. Everyone would want a piece of it. Then they thought they could mail it home and keep it. But that was wishful thinking. Finally they ended up realizing that the only decent way was to report finding it and turn it over to the authorities. "All the schemes were impractical," said the lieutenant. "I went out and called the helicopter. It came and picked up the box, and you know something funny? We never heard any mention of that gold again!"

Tunnel searchers never knew what they might find. Sometimes it was not as exciting as uncovering a cache of gold bars. Sometimes they wondered what might be in those stone jugs buried and hidden in side chambers. One wonders how many of those were dug up and the contents examined for hidden treasure.

It was better if you had an experienced tunnel guide at hand to brief you on what might be hidden in those side chambers. They could tell you that those who lived for years in these tunnels resolved the question of where to eliminate their waste by having separate chambers where they buried large stoneware jugs. These were used as their latrines until one was full. Its mouth was then closed off with earth and another jug was used. In most cases this luxury was not available for everyone, so one just dug a hole where they were, did their business and then covered it up. Another surprise booby trap for tunnel explorers.

Also there were times when they hurriedly dragged their dead soldiers down into the tunnels. This was done for two reasons. One, it was very repugnant to the Vietnamese to leave a body unburied. Also by bringing the bodies into the tunnel with them they figured it frustrated Americans who they knew were making body counts. They then buried the bodies in a fetus position in the walls of the tunnel covered by a few inches of clay. Supposedly after the war these would be brought out and given a proper burial. They also dragged into the tunnels bodies of American soldiers so their comrades were psychologically demoralized by not knowing what happened to them. Occasionally they never had time to bury the bodies and tunnel rats reported the horror and stench of having to crawl through that rotting flesh.

The job of tunnel rat was not one for anyone who was even slightly claustrophobic. One of the military commanders described it as hot, dirty, and gasping for breath, he squeezed his body through narrow and shallow openings on all fours, never knowing whether the tunnel might collapse behind him or what he might find ahead around the next turn, and sensing the jolt of adrenaline at every sound. Surely this modern combat spelunker (cave explorer) is a special breed. Another officer said there is nothing more curious than an American soldier, particularly if he thinks there's an enemy down there somewhere. "I found in each company when it went out into an area of tunnels the tunnel rat became a sort of oddball hero. You had guys that took great pride in showing their buddies they were unique in terms of courage. It's amazing what human beings will do in that sort of situation."

Another officer admitted that it took a special kind of being that had to have an inquisitive mind, plenty of guts, and a real understanding as to what not to touch and what you could touch in order to stay alive. Because if you didn't keep your eyes open all the time you could get into trouble in a hurry.

When the brass realized how extensive these tunnels were and how often the enemy disappeared into them, they tried to make up teams of tunnel rats all over the place. But they quickly found that too many of them were being killed by the Viet Cong because they did not know how to avoid the kind of problems they got into.

Infantrymen, who were volunteers or ordered to go down into the tunnels, sometimes met death in some strange ways. The Viet Cong's favorite method was to slit a man's throat or to strangle them with a garrote as he came up through a tunnel's trap door.

When squads of tunnel rats were organized, wise officers took only volunteers. Early on they realized that if they ordered someone into a tunnel and they were fearful for their lives the man was often so freaked out he popped back out in a hurry to report that the tunnel went only ten or twelve feet and that was the end of it.

Even the volunteers who had experience in the tunnels sometimes had a panic attack and ended up screaming as they double-timed to the exit and got the heck out of there.

No officer liked to have his people underground for too long a time. If he detected any sign of panic in them they were ordered to stay out of the tunnels. Dead or wounded rats were never abandoned. Someone always went in and recovered their bodies, or in some cases they had lifelines attached to them so that if anything happened their buddies could drag them out. Since all of these tunnels were built by smaller people, large-framed soldiers simply could not fit into the tunnels. Because of that requirement many of the men who volunteered for the job were smaller, lightweights. Many were Hispanic – Porto Rican or Mexican.

In the years that followed the more popular the tunnel rats became the more they had their own badge. One of which shows a gray rodent holding a pistol in one hand and a flashlight in the other. The Latin phrase underneath is *Non Gratum Anus Rodentum* that supposedly translates to "Not Acceptable Alive" but the tunnel rats translate it as "Not Worth a Rat's Ass."

In one division each company had a tunnel rat. Officers were not permitted to enter any of the tunnels. Tunnel rats were all volunteers. The reason for volunteering for this kind of hazardous duty ranged from resolving problems that they had back home to using this as a way to prove their manhood in front of their peers. For some, the adrenal rush plus the surrounding protection of the tunnel walls comforted some of them who preferred the silence of the tunnel where warfare was reduced to a one-on-one combat situation. Those who embraced the darkness of the grave-like interior relished the idea that in some cases the light at the end of the tunnel often came from an enemy's candle and they were the ones about to snuff it out.

One officer recalled one of his tunnel rats who was a skinny boy with lots of pimples, pale-faced, gung ho type eager to get down into the tunnels and find the enemy. He was doing this when his buddies on top heard a shot ring out from inside the tunnel. When they got to him he had been wounded. They brought him out and put him in the hospital. When his CO went to see him he realized the boy could hardly wait to get back into the tunnels again.

Another tunnel rat they called Private Little was doing his duty about 40 feet back inside a tunnel when he found a trap door that led down into another level. As he lifted it a booby trap went off triggering a cave-in on him.

He was buried face down with only his feet sticking out. His rescuers tied ropes to his feet and tried to drag him out but couldn't. They had to dig down from the top. He was about twelve feet down. It took thirty minutes of extremely frantic digging before they got to where they saw his feet and they were wriggling! He was still alive because his hands covered his face and he was able to barely breathe but with extreme difficulty.

He was only semi-conscious when they finally dug him out and sent him to the hospital. As soon as he came to, he discharged himself. The hospital thought he had gone AWOL and sent the military police looking for him. But in fact Private Little came straight back to his unit anxious to get back into the tunnels again. Private Little's idea of R&R was to stay on patrol hoping to find more tunnels for him to search.

Like all tunnel rats, these men were a special breed. They had an especially deadly task to perform that set them apart from the rest of the grunts. It was said by those who knew, that of all the U.S. servicemen in Vietnam, only the Long Range Reconnaissance Teams (LRPS) and helicopter pilots had such close brushes with mortal danger and consistently enjoyed that reputation.

Tunnel Rats that were good at what they did and who survived because they were that good, did not hesitate to kill. They were loners who gained respect from the men they soldiered with because they constantly took on missions no other soldier would even consider doing. Some of these killers were aggressive types with possibly criminal or almost criminal backgrounds and quite possibly pretty dark motives for doing what they did. While others were completely normal, well-balanced soldiers who performed their duty well. But at times that duty in the tunnels so scarred their subconscious minds that they were never able to forget the nightmares they lived.

Every rat had their own way of doing things, their own choice of tunnel gear they felt comfortable with and especially their own preference of weapons. Their two most important items were their light and their weapon. If their light failed at a critical time they could be in deep do-do. So they carried spare bulbs and practiced changing them in the dark while in their crawl position. They had to do this sight unseen while juggling in their other hand a heavy U.S. Army issue Colt .45. Its impressive bark inside that three-foot wide clay tunnel was going to knock out their hearing and put a roar in their head that was so loud it would disturb their sleep.

Every rat carried some kind of light. It was always a question of how he carried it and whether or not he kept it on or off and what he would do if he dropped it and broke the bulb. Some preferred having a light attached to their head to free one hand while the other carried a handgun. But then they became aware that a light created a target and they sure didn't like the idea of that target being their head. Some carried a hand-light that they could turn off most of the time as they crawled along the passageway. But if they did that they didn't know when there was a booby trap either hanging from the ceiling or right in front of them.

The other thing that became quite personal was the kind of weapon they chose to carry. Some went for a handgun with less of a bang. Others however, chose a weapon with more bang. Few of the rats wanted the big handgun, which was too big, too cumbersome and too loud. They preferred to choose their own pistol. One they felt more comfortable with. In some cases that was a Smith and Wesson .38. Another rat felt more comfortable with a German Lugar, while another used an Italian .25 Beretta. The idea of putting silencers on their handguns was not popular because it lengthened their barrels and made the handgun more cumbersome to handle.

If a tunnel rat took a rifle into a tunnel he chose a captured AK-47 figuring its firing would be recognized by the VC as one of their own.

Interestingly some rats opt for sawed off shotguns in the small calibers. Their large scatter pattern of pellets guaranteed a hit. But that much explosion in tight quarters would just about wipe out one's hearing from that day on. One rat got hold of an M-2 carbine with a paratrooper's stock that folded up to a 22 inches length.

Even small thin really limber tunnel rats found that they could barely squeeze through some of the openings made by the small Vietnamese builders; in fact the zigzags built into the communication tunnels were so tight that some of our skinny rats said they had difficulty getting around them.

Occasionally there was another danger: A rat would go down into a tunnel to explore it, getting himself sweaty, dirty, his clothes messed up and his hair disheveled while his buddies hung around outside the tunnel waiting to hear how he was. If it happened to be time to break for lunch they would move off and take that break. Meanwhile another group of soldiers might come by and check out the mouth of the tunnel. Right then is when our scruffy, dirty, smelly tunnel rat decides to pop out expecting to see his buddies.

But what he sees instead is a bunch of angry faces looking at him over the sights of their M-16s while our scared rat is talking double-time about who he is and who the president is and what the score is of the most recent ball game. One more reason why tunnel ratting was a very precarious business.

Today, decades after the Vietnam War, the Vietnamese people have turned their incredible tunnel systems into popular tourist attractions. I have never met a tunnel rat who has the slightest interest in re-visiting them.

7

Lifer, You're a Good Dog, You

As Point Man, Short Round had already checked it out.
The village looked peaceful. After he reported this, the
platoon moved up to the clearing in the bamboo where
several hooches were built. Old women stood outside their
huts talking while old men were gathered around a fire pit
roasting something. The platoon's guide talked to the natives
and they said they had not seen any VC in the area for almost
a month. Suddenly a small black and brown dog came
running for its life toward them with an old man hot on her
heels. The pup stopped in front of their CO and looked up at
him. The Old Man reached down and scooped her up into his
arms. He said sharply to the old man chasing her, "She's mine
now. Go get something else to eat!" The dog-chaser moved off
grumbling.

The Vietnamese have no pets. Everything with four legs
gets eaten. Dog is high on their menu. Their guide told them
that the pup's mother was what the men were roasting over
their fire.

Their CO said, "Your name is 'Lifer' now and you will
take care of our company."

Apparently that was okay with the pooch because she was
vigorously licking the Old Man's grinning face.

No little dog ever got so much loving from every man in
their company. Nobody missed a chance to pet or play with
the feisty little dog. Each and every one of them loved her
because she reminded them of home and the dogs they grew

up with and had loved too.

Best of all she had so much dislike for those who had done what they did to her family that she stiffened, bristled and growled whenever she knew the Vietnamese were around. She didn't have to see them, Lifer sensed or smelled them. She was like an early warning system. She let them know even at night whenever the enemy was near.

Short Round continued on with his tunnel rat activities and they had many more Search and Clear missions but most of them never amounted to anything. Then came a day when they hit a jackpot – there were tunnels everywhere but no sign of Charlie.

As he had found out from earlier experiences, that often meant nothing.

So, once again Short Round prepared himself to do down into the tunnels. He got rid of everything including his dog tags and stripped down for action. But this time the company's extra special little dog the CO named Lifer stood by his side ready to go with him. Lifer had been adopted by the company, mainly because they all loved her but especially because she was such a good warning system that Charlie was somewhere nearby. She never failed them. Whenever the little dog would stiffen up with every hair on her body standing at attention, soldiers knew at once that the enemy was coming.

The little dog had never been down in a tunnel before. Not that she didn't always dance around them begging to go. But Short Round always said no to the little dog as he did now. "No, sweetheart, you can't go."

The Top said, "Awww, let her go."

But understandably, Short Round was not comfortable with that idea at all. He was well aware that the little dog could give him away. But then he thought, maybe not. She has always been the perfect one to let us know in advance when Charlie was around. So, he said, "Well okay, Babe. This one time."

When Lifer realized she was included in the hunt for the

bad guys, she was beside herself. Everybody could tell that she was excited about the prospects because she was grinning from ear to ear.

Top grinned after the little tunnel rat and his equally small helper. He grinned and called, "Good for you, Short Round! Every Rat needs a good dog and you got a winnah!"

"Thanks," the Rat called over his shoulder. Then he and the dog squirmed down through the tunnel opening.

Just a short distance further and they found themselves in an enormous underground chamber with tunnel openings all over the place. There were individual rooms everywhere but there wasn't a single sign of a human being ever being in the tunnel. It looked old and abandoned. But it sure had been busy at one time.

Short Round and his sidekick kept moving on. After about fifteen minutes of moving slowly through the dark passageway and finding nothing, Short Round suddenly heard Lifer growling at his side in the darkness.

That instantly started the Rat's adrenal glands pumping, realizing now that the dog's growling would surely give away his position. That was all he needed to have a Viet Cong come charging out of the darkness if only because he thought he was about to catch himself a canine dinner.

But in the dark Short Round couldn't see the little dog. Instead he stopped even breathing, listening as hard as he could to the silence. The Rat's light was clipped on his belt. He slowly eased his left hand down until he touched Lifer's back. The dog's fur was standing up and she was doing a slow stiff-legged prance. He eased his finger up against her throat and felt the low growl she was making. Neither of them moved a muscle. Then, suddenly she bolted forward in a rush. At the same time Short Round saw a flash and heard gunfire from two feet away … a Cong soldier was in the darkness directly ahead of them and he shot at the dog!

Short Round pointed and pulled the trigger of his .45. After the explosion, he heard the thud of a body hitting the ground.

The first thing he did was turn on his flashlight to make sure he was completely dead. He was. "Dead as a doornail," thought Short Round and instantly it flashed through his mind, *"But where is Lifer?"*

In a panic he flashed his light beam into every corner of the darkness on both sides of him, scared but not wanting to think about it that maybe she had been shot and killed!

Then suddenly the little dog put her front paws on his leg and he looked down and saw her looking up at him showing her teeth in a wide smile and wagging her tail at him.

"Oh, thank God," he whispered. He dropped his hand down and swiftly petted her. She licked it. "What a *great* dog," he thought. *Lifer had just saved his life!*

They both came back up out of the hole and Top was right there to greet them. He listened to Short Round's story while Top roughhoused with the excited little dog.

"You guys are the best!" he said. "And we've got some more tunnels over here," he pointed.

Short Round's response never made it to his lips but he thought it, *"Sure. Why not?"*

8

Where There Were Brave Heroes
There Was Hope

So he wriggled his way down into another one, this time
leaving Lifer, the feisty dog, behind. He wasn't sure if dogs
had as many lives as cats, but he sure didn't want to take a
chance on that.

This tunnel was like the others – hot, stinking, humid, and
pitch black. What was sitting there in this inky stinking hole
waiting for him? His heart was hammering already and he
tried not to breathe so hard. Anybody in there, sitting in that
blackness with his clammy hands wrapped around the slimy
stock of an AK-47, would hear him coming from a mile away.
Slow down, he told himself as he crept forward, trying to sense
any danger that might be ahead of him. Now he wished he'd
have brought the little dog. Lifer could smell them long before
Short Round could key in on their fishy scent. That's how the
little dog had warned him in the tunnel before. But now, as
usual, he was alone again, the way all tunnel rats were.

The .45 he clutched in his right hand felt heavier and
clumsier than usual and the damn thing was slick from his
sweat already. Par for the course, thought Short Round ...
Slow down, damnit! His heart was still racing and he pursed his
dry lips trying to get his panting under control. *Damnit, slow
down ....*

Using the same technique that he always used for safety's
sake, he kept his flashlight turned off while he moved through

the darkness, turning it on for maybe three seconds to get his bearings then switching it off while he inched slowly through the darkness.

He always counted on his sharp hearing when he couldn't see what was ahead of him but now after his recent experience with the VC, his ears were doing their usual roaring and he felt like he was again underwater. That roaring and not hearing could get him killed. That thought did nothing but pump another jolt of adrenaline into his already hyper system.

As he inched along he began to realize that this tunnel had more turns to it than a snake. He had gone about a hundred feet when he suddenly realized that he could see a dim light far ahead of him. So he continued on toward the light in the distance, trying to move as cautiously as possible.

When he was a few feet from the light and was aiming at it with his .45 he suddenly realized that no one was there!

"What the –!" He snapped on his flashlight.

As he turned he felt the hard cold muzzle of an AK-47 pressed against his forehead!

Short Round's whole life flashed before him. He saw his sobbing wife at home clutching their new-borne son who was unable to understand why his mother was crying.

In the light he saw the man was wearing the uniform of the North Vietnamese Army. Now he knew how he managed to sneak up behind him because those soldiers were much better trained that the Viet Cong.

A tight smile spread across the man's dark face. His black eyes glittered as he said something to him. Short Round would have given anything to know what he said. All he knew was that this nightmare was probably one he would never wake up from … and then surprisingly he heard the soldier's rifle click.

Short Round instantly responded to the soldier's jammed weapon. Four fast shots rang out from his .45 and it was all over. No telling how many angels were sitting on Short Round's shoulder during that encounter but he was shaking so hard and sweating so profusely that when he crawled out of that tunnel he looked as though he had fallen into a rice paddy.

The Top looked at him with an expression of pure fright on his face. "My God," he said to Short Round, "You're white as a sheet!"

Short Round's reply was short and to the point. "I'm done, Top. No more, ever again. I'm done!" Top grinned back at him with a crooked smile and said, "You never should have started, son." Still smiling he nodded in agreement to Short Round's final grown-up decision.

But was he really? Was he really done?

This part of Jonathon Jones book, *Beneath the Bamboo: a Vietnam War Story* is important enough to be included exactly as he wrote it. It gives readers some idea of how much these things meant to our men at war.

I told Top I was done for the day, and he said that it was no problem, especially since we had a show to go see.

The choppers picked us up, and it seemed like we were in flight for thirty minutes. We finally landed at Phu Cat, and we were beyond jacked. The Bob Hope show — how cool was that?

When we arrived at our destination, we noticed a big stage, but it seemed a million miles away. Seated for many rows were hundreds of Air Force personnel dressed in all of their pretty blue uniforms. You should have seen the look on their faces when they turned around and saw the infantry fully dressed in combat gear, with dirty fatigues that looked like they had never been washed, scruffy beards, and bad ass attitudes due to what we had been through. We were really far back, but we didn't care because we were really happy to be out of that jungle.

After about twenty or thirty minutes, Bob Hope comes out on stage and everyone starts clapping and hollering. Then he lays it all on the line, and to this day what he did made me have more respect and admiration for the man when compared to any celebrity who has ever lived.

"You Air Force guys. I love you to death, but the show will not start until you move back and let the army infantry guys be up front."

He knew fully well by the way we looked that we were in the

thick of it, and that is why he felt we deserved to see the show closer than any other.

Thankfully, there was no animosity from them. They were completely willing to do as Mr. Hope suggested. So there I was, a combat-stricken young man from the middle of a giant corn field, now in the front row of a show that contained one of the most famous comedians of our time.

When the show began, Bob did his usual comedy routine. Then Joey Heatherton came out and did a little dance. Next, the main attraction for me, and most of the others, was Raquel Welch. When she came out on stage the whistling didn't stop for fifteen minutes.

This was the second most beautiful woman I had ever seen in my life, with my wife being the first. [*The sexy pinup photo she gave him was signed 'Love, Raquel Welch.'*] Overall, it was like we were in another world, far away from the place that we had to wake up to every day.

After an hour and a half it ended, and when we departed, all of the Air Force guys stood up and they all began clapping for us. That meant everything to us. It really did. During this one brief moment, we were all dropped into what seemed like a dreamy fantasy world, but once it was all over with we were quickly put back into the face of reality. Sadly, all of the choppers picked us up and dropped us off into the jungle once again.

Bottom line, Short Round not only survived the war but here's how he ended his memoir of it:

Once my name came up, (the Inspecting General) stated, "I see in your files that you've been awarded many honors, with the bronze star for valor, and clusters to go with it. In addition, you got the combat infantry badge and the air medal."

Knowing he was getting at something, I knew I had to see what he was getting at. "What do you want, sir? Because those things don't mean crap to me."

"I'm willing to give you $10,000 to re-up," he firmly replied.

I responded to his offer as kindly as I could. "Sir, with all due respect, the army can kiss my ass. The answer is no."

Shocked, but still holding a firm gaze, he said, "Well, the others said the same thing, but they were a little kinder with their reply."

But I didn't care. Sending a young man who was constantly

trying to prove himself and be brave into another deadly game of life roulette wasn't something I would care to repeat. I did my time, I served my country, and I learned my lessons well.

MORE TUNNEL TALES
From Vietnam

1

Weasel's Flight

Well into the war an outfit called Wergen's Tunnel Rats
got such a good reputation for cleaning out tunnels that they
soon were in demand to do likewise in other areas. So, they
began to expand their operation. Since they had to take on
more people they started recruiting by word and by radio to
other units, asking for volunteers who wanted to become part
of this elite operation. They were told that if they qualified to
join this prestigious group they would gain respect from all of
their comrades.

One of those volunteers who easily made the grade
certainly had the build for it. His name was Wally Carter who
hailed from the Midwest. Thanks to Wally's string-bean build
and his ability to wiggle through the smallest tunnel openings
everyone fondly called him "Weasel."

On one of the Rat's routine tunnel trips near Cu Chi they
came upon a tunnel with an extremely small entranceway and
a deeply slanting descent into the black abyss. Naturally this
was Weasel's cup of tea. But it was such a steeply descending
narrow tunnel and no one crawls backwards comfortably if
they have to come out quickly, the other team-members came

up with an idea for a rapid extraction method if Weasel should get into trouble.

They tied a rope to his ankles, backed a jeep up to the entranceway and tied the other end of the rope to the jeep. With a .45 caliber Colt in one hand and a prod to probe for booby traps in the other, Weasel squirmed through the tight tunnel entry.

Slowly in the dark he worked his way down the steep shaft, quietly feeling the tunnel floor ahead of him for anything unusual. He moved in the dark like a big Inch Worm. Naturally he was sweating up a storm and hyperventilating, but he tried to be as quiet as possible.

Topside his buddies held their breaths, sweated bullets for their brave buddy and carefully paid out the rope as he moved slowly along.

It was a long, deep shaft and he was a long ways into it. The jeep was slowly backed up so that there was always a short length of slack between Weasel's lifeline and the rear end of the jeep. The driver kept the motor idling and in gear with the clutch depressed.

Suddenly the group's straining ears heard muffled shots underground followed by Weasel's frantic screams for help. The jeep driver popped the clutch, the jeep lurched forward and after some difficulty and tunnel noises sounding like a muffled toilet being flushed, Weasel shot out of the tunnel feet first, still clutching his .45 in his right hand and his prod in his left hand. He bounced a couple times through the jungle undergrowth before his buddies caught up to him, but they were glad to see that he was still in one long string-bean piece and hadn't left more than some scraped skin behind.

Of course after the shock he'd had and the somewhat bumpy ride back to the surface Weasel's eyes were the size of golf balls. He gasped so hard he couldn't talk for awhile. But as they untied him and dabbed his scrapes with disinfectants, he managed to gasp out his story.

He said he came to a trap door in the floor and as he was

prodding around its edges it suddenly dropped open and he was staring down at five heavily armed thunderstruck Viet Cong soldiers sitting around a crude table eating a meal by lantern-light.

For an instant both parties stared bug-eyed at each other. Then, mayhem!

In the excitement Weasel got off two shots and screamed for extraction as the VC grabbed for their AK-47s. He said his ride up the tunnel was a little like being shot out of a cannon backwards, but thanks to their swift response he made it in one piece.

Weasel was the Rats' hero from that day on. They swiftly sent down some C4 explosives for the enemies underground, but everyone knew that all those guys were interested in was putting as much tunnel distance and trap doors as possible between themselves and those crazy American Tunnel Rats.

2

Thank You, Mr. Informant

The Allies once thought that the tunnels were limited in their length and if we pumped enough gas or water into the entrances we could flood them and take out any enemy hiding there. Too often though whenever we got brave enough to send a small soldier down into those depths wearing a gas mask he often found no one there. No bodies at all. Now how had they pulled that off?

One of the best-kept secrets that the Viet Cong had was that they had built exit tunnels all over their tunnel system so that there were many ways out. Since not many soldiers were willing to go down and see what remained of the enemy after they pumped the gas into a tunnel, we never realized that sometimes none of the enemy was being killed. As soon as they realized their tunnel had been discovered they headed back through the escape system of secret side passages and disappeared.

When our artillery shellings and aerial bombardments increased in intensity the Viet Cong had to modify their tunnels so they would provide more protection. They purposely made cone or A-shaped tunnels now so that they resisted the high-explosives going off at ground level. What they didn't realize, but learned, was that this cone-shaped tunnel acted as an underground amplifier and magnified the approaching B-52 strikes. This was the only air raid warning these tunnel people had in advance of any aerial attack. It saved many of their lives.

Quite quickly the enemy realized that the only way they

could keep their tunnels hidden was to make their camouflage so good that their entrances would not be discovered.

One of their captured documents told tunnel dwellers in one area that they should grow live plants and make sure they were secured firmly to the entrance covers on their tunnels. If there were any dried leaves that would make them stand out they should be removed and replaced with green ones. All these things had to be done before daybreak, otherwise such small details, that could be detected by the Green Berets who were specially trained in these areas, would call attention to these places by their contrast. Also they were told not to leave any piles of dirt from their tunnel digging because they would be a sure give-away. That dirt should be dumped into a bomb crater or a river. Nothing should suggest that there might be a tunnel in the area.

Unbeknownst to the enemy, we had an informant that the intelligence people had working inside the VC. In July 1967 he told his handlers that, despite the clever camouflaging of the tunnel entrances, American soldiers could be trained in how to find the tunnels. He told them to look for evidence of trails. Broken branches, crushed grasses or any such things that disturbed the natural growth might be an indication of a tunnel nearby. The idea of the tunnels was to provide shelter for their troops, especially during the daytime when large numbers of them might be spotted by our aerial surveillance. So it was extremely important that everything connected with the tunnels be made to look as natural as their jungle surroundings.

In some areas, such as the Cu Chi district northwest of Saigon in southern Vietnam where we had our large base camp, the enemy had many tunnels, but not all of them were in use. How were the Americans expected to know which ones were deadly and which ones were just plain dead?

One canny Tunnel Rat had a system. Here's what he said:

"Often when you pop the lid on one of these places and look down into the tunnel, the first thing you may see are about ten thousand silver eyes looking back at you. Spider eyes! If you see nothing but unbroken spider webs it's a deserted tunnel. If you see few spiders and lots of broken webs the tunnel has been used recently. If there are no spiders and no webs look for scratch marks because it will be a new tunnel or one getting plenty of recent use."

The fellow added: "If you are a tunnel rat going into it, carry a pistol with a silencer, a small flashlight, and a prod for booby traps. To carry all that you need a third hand. Otherwise you stick your light on your head and wonder if all you are doing is lighting it up for the enemy down there who will try to turn it off."

For serious Tunnel Rats they solved the lighted target problem by keeping their lights out and letting their eyes adjust to the darkness while their ears became their primary warning system.

In his book *Into the Abyss: The Elite Tunnel Rats,* author Riley St. James describes Tunnel Rat development in September 1967 at the Di-An Base where explosives expert Sergeant Thomas Wergen took over what he described as a loosely organized group of tunnel rats.

Before the Americans knew about this underground world they searched for the enemy on the surface, bombing and shelling it to pieces while entire battalions of the enemy waited patiently underground. As author St. James described it:

> The earth cracked and groaned, and in places gave way. The landscape changed from jungle to dusty desert; entire villages disappeared and the inhabitants were moved out. But the physical integrity of the tunnels was to survive long enough for a shadow civilian and military communist administration to live in the tunnels, conducting its business and defying nearly every attempt to force it up and out. It was an extraordinary triumph of the primitive in a decade that saw a man walking on the moon.

3

Wergen's Rats

It was late afternoon. So late it was getting on toward chow time and the shadows that moved through the under-story in single file moved faster than usual, each man separated from one another by half a dozen paces so that if one tripped a booby trap it wouldn't take out three of them.

The under-story jungle darkened long before daylight departed but as the foot soldiers gingerly picked their way through the foliage, they were completely alone. Everything around them including the earth under their boots could have belonged to the dead. No one made a sound. Their movements were not normal. Even the jungle sounds quieted as the patrol slipped past in the direction of an LZ on a knoll. Had anyone been listening – and they were – the sound of a distant helicopter coming in and then departing, was not lost to the listeners.

Long after they were gone, the jungle remained still as though traumatized by their silent passing. But after a long pause that under-story world slowly changed.

Once night fell totally, that subterranean world of silence began to buzz with life. And it was not all from the insect world. First came Dien Bien Phu Kitchens, the so-called smokeless variety had been introduced to Vietnam when they were used in the trenches during the war against the French. Now however, they had been refined and were used by the underground world of Vietnam.

The silent jungle gradually picked up the scent of smoke, but none was visible as the Dien Bien Phu chimneys were widely separated and cleverly concealed at ground level where the smoke was broadly distributed and invisible. But no one could miss that smoky aroma. The system was described as being smokeless, but those who lived underground in confinement knew otherwise. They could hardly wait for the Americans to clear out of an area so they could come up for a breath of fresh air and cook their raw rice in small hidden places using these tiny stoves. Whenever possible the rice was supplemented with grilled tunnel rat much cherished by the Vietnamese who said that it had a better flavor than chicken or duck.

In September 1967, explosives specialist Sergeant Thomas Wergen became part of the 168th Combat Engineers stationed at Di-An where he was soon assigned to take over a small group of Tunnel Rats. He found that the guys had the guts for the job but they lacked the experience. All of them had been in Nam for some time though. One of them already had seven campaign ribbons. He was a character named Robert Cornell dubbed "Cowboy" because he loved riding into battle astride a bouncing jeep firing an M-60 machine gun like a cowboy on a horse shooting Indians. Cornell had been the longest in country and Wergen felt that he could count on him. Next, with slightly less experience in the group was Jim Dunning who they called Monkey Man because he scampered around inside the tunnels like an agile monkey. He too was a no-nonsense kind that Wergen knew he could count on. So Wergen, Cornell and Dunning comprised the core of what would turn out to be Wergen's Dream Team of Tunnel Rats.

Using the local tunnels to practice in, the sergeant started training them on the tactics that they were to perfect. With basic equipment and plenty of determination the group began to fine-tune their operation.

Usually when they found a new tunnel they used no flashlights at first because they only made them better targets. Instead, as soon as they got inside the main tunnel each of the men learned to depend on their natural night vision. What they also instinctively developed was a heightened ability to hear and smell. Even the slightest sounds of rustling clothes were magnified in the dark. If someone was in there with them, they quickly knew it. The other sense they developed to a high degree was their sense of smell. The Vietnamese's main diet of rice and smelly dried fish gave them an invisible aroma that no American mistook for anything but one of them. [The same went for the VC who said they always knew when an American was around when they whiffed perfumed soap or shaving lotion. Recruits quickly learned not to use any of that stuff.] But the Vietnamese never could avoid the fishy giveaway.

Wergen's Rats' choice of weapons varied. At first they carried a .22 automatic pistol equipped with a silencer to try to avoid damaging their eardrums during shootouts in the tight tunnel confines. But they quickly learned that the enemy usually used heavier weapons and the Rats scraped their pea-shooter .22s in favor of sawed-off .30 caliber M-2 Carbines. If a tunnel appeared to be especially dangerous they carried .45 caliber "Grease Guns" [Small submachine-guns resembling a mechanic's grease gun.] with silencers. They did the job. But these weapons proved too big and bulky to be dragged through the tunnels regularly; so a handgun or an M-2 Carbine was their usual weapon of choice.

Some of the tunnels were easy to find; others were not. Some were the standard tunnels dug by people dragging baskets of earth and using short-handled hoes. Once they filled a basket they passed it to those behind them to extract the earth. These were usually the 10 to 20 foot long tunnels 2 to 4 feet wide. Little more than man-sized hide-outs designed to conceal snipers with maybe their simple living supplies and weapons.

Where these tunnels were dug, the excavated earth was usually scattered on the surface somewhere. In weeks, these small mounds of earth would take on a natural layer of green growth and blend in with the landscape. Earthen mounds were the kind of places American soldiers were told to look for because in a normally flat area they would look out of place.

Wergen found that some of the complex tunnels were incredibly well designed. These often had several well camouflaged entrances and they were large enough underground to accommodate large numbers of Viet Cong troops for extended periods of warfare. Scattered near these tunnels were elaborate air ducts that were small and hard to find at ground level because they were often placed under a shrub at the base of its main trunk, or some less obvious place such as behind the corner post of a pig sty. (Guess what that air smelled like?) Such disgusting places were often selected by the VC to be good sites for tunnel entrances because no one would likely be poking around in a pile of pig excrement looking for anything.

When his men wondered why some of the tunnels were so simple while others were extremely complex Wergen told them, "You have to remember that the Vietnamese people have literally been at war since the 1940s beginning with the Japanese. They've had enough experience digging these tunnels that they're masters at it by now."

He pointed out that the kind of tunnel soil was called laterite, which was loaded with red iron and aluminum. When exposed to air it turned as hard as concrete. Thanks to this, their tunnels needed no shoring up with timber posts and lintels. The only place where the Rats ever found any wood in a tunnel was around its entrance and around the many trapdoors. He said that in over 900 tunnels they never found any type of shoring to support the walls or ceilings of these shafts. Not even when the most complex of these tunnel systems were found to be miles long and eight stories deep.

How the Americans learned about the whereabouts of the tunnels was usually accidental. They were reported by the troops who stumbled across them sometimes when the camouflaging foliage was knocked off during the construction of a base camp or airfield.

In time, most of the enemy's significant tunnels were discovered and "denied" as they called it, through the efforts of the diligent tunnel hunters of the 27th LCT (land-clearing task force) that Wergen was assigned to.

Once they were in an area known to be riddled with tunnels, they called in a 25-ton bulldozer with a special oversized blade called a Rhone Plow that simply scalped everything it was used on, thereby uncovering many of the concealed entryways,

But no one was quick to take them out as they once were with grenades down their entryways. Not after a number of tunnels turned out to be storage areas for land mines. When a grenade set them off, everyone in the area went up with them. Hence, always the precaution of looking before destroying.

In the course of searching these tunnels, the team found some interesting things. There was always the possibility that the tunnels contained important supplies, usually firearms or stashes of rice; on occasion important intelligence. The Tunnel Rats never knew what actually might be awaiting them in that dark tunnel underground. They expected booby traps and possibly even poisonous jungle critters. Wergen once was bitten by a tunnel spider the size of a teacup and ended up with a badly infected hand. A field doctor opened it up and slathered it with medication without bothering to give him any kind of painkiller.

The tunnels were not just a straight tube either. There were variations to them. And there were trapdoors along the way that were intended to trap any invaders. Here's how the team worked:

They were usually three man teams in their initial search for tunnels. Each man in the team had specific tasks. Of course their one basic priority was to constantly keep their eyes on each other's back during this high tension time when each man's adrenaline system was working overtime.

With fragging (blowing it with a fragmentation grenade) a thing of the past, the usual first reaction of a new tunnel rat to a new tunnel was to drop down into the hole not knowing what lay ahead. With his non-participating buddies watching his every move he tried to brave it out, but his breathing gave him away. Most new rats panted like a hound running a rabbit. They were often so scared that they were out of breath for a moment. When they realized they had made it that far they calmed themselves, put their sensing systems on high alert and went on to do their job.

The point man of course was the one who had the most difficult task of confronting whatever dangers lurked there. He had to make sure there was no hidden explosive device in front of them. He carefully felt for a trip wire and checked out anything that felt suspicious to his touch. Such traps could be as simple but devilishly clever as a sudden sharp angle in the side wall where a deadly King cobra snake might be stashed with its tail securely tied to a stake. Nothing restricted his deadly reach. Whatever was there, the front man got to deal with it first. The man following him stayed a good 15 feet behind the point man because that was the kill range of an accidentally tripped Coke can grenade. The group members took turns being the point man so each of them got to share that risk.

The second man behind the first checked the tunnel walls for hollow places or loosely covered disguises that concealed openings to other tunnels.

The third man stayed fifteen feet back from the second, searched the ceiling and floor of the tunnel for false openings. They knew that sometimes the Viet Cong installed trapdoors in the floor or ceiling of a tunnel that might open onto another level, or be a deadly trap.

Some of these were cleverly designed traps made to catch intruders. Some were triggered to spring open directly behind the unsuspecting intruder. Other trapdoors were made to lock in place trapping the person who had just crawled pass. The invader was helpless because in his cramped position he was unable to turn around. It was just a matter of time before he ran out of air and died there.

Other trapdoors were made to pop open suddenly like a Jack-in-the-Box to reveal a very lively VC wielding either a knife, a bayonet, or firing a handgun.

Probably some of the more high tension times for the rats were during a search where the three of them would enter a much larger tunnel and find that the passageway forked and went off in different directions. Usually the team separated and explored both tunnels. As their eyes tried to penetrate the darkness and their ears strained for any sounds of danger, they bravely crawled on praying that nothing would happen. If the tunnel proved to be circular they knew that sooner or later in the darkness they would either run into one of their nervous trigger-happy buddies or an equally nervous trigger- or slash-happy enemy soldier. Which was it to be? That's the way you get frayed nerves in a hurry. And if you jumped the gun it might be your buddy you blew away in the dark.

Talk about rough stuff! They had only a split second to decide which kind of action they would use. Fortunately not many of the tunnels were circular and created this problem. Usually when they forked passageways moved off in different directions and might end up in huge supply rooms or places where large numbers of troops could sleep out the day and go out another exit when night fell.

After the tunnels were discovered and any intelligence or supplies or armaments were completely removed, the last thing they did was to obliterate the tunnels. Usually it was with high explosives. In some cases they set 10-pound bags of tear gas powder along the passageways linked with detonating cord every 20 or 30 feet. Then it would be set off from outside. The powerful explosion would embed the tear gas powder into the tunnel walls where its poisonous effects would remain for about 20 years. That pretty much assured that there would be no human use of that tunnel system again.

4

Special Training

Based on real people and real events in my book *Tunnel Tales from Vietnam,* I described an American soldier who earned the nickname "Short Round." He had shouted that warning as a mortar round misfired and fell back on his group. Fortunately it was a dud or everyone would have been killed.

Proud of his Nam nickname, Short Round becomes a hero to his buddies because he always volunteers for the extremely dangerous job of being the company Tunnel Rat, a job only smaller people could do. That was because the tunnel builders purposely built these hidden entry and escape routes to fit only their small statures. With but few exceptions, all the allies were too big to fit into the tunnels. Just the way the tunnel builders planned it.

What I didn't reveal in that first book is what Short Round attributed his drive to become someone people looked up to and respected. He felt that since he was small, slightly built and shy, he would never be what people then thought he-men looked like. So how did he muster the courage, determination and drive to take on this highly perilous job as a tunnel rat?

Short Round believed that how people conducted themselves in high stress situations where they could lose their lives, depended on lessons they learned growing up. Could they tough it out, or would they give up? He never really understood that until his Vietnam War experiences.

Just after World War II at the age of two, his parents divorced. A few years later his mom met and married someone else. He was a World War II veteran. When the boy first met his stepfather the man seemed extremely cold and bitter toward the world in general. Short Round described the man as being built like a bulldog with the disposition of a grizzly bear whose cubs had just been stolen.

The boy lived in fear of the man throughout his entire childhood. His stepfather was a lifetime Army veteran, highly decorated with ribbons and medals, after having been a longtime prisoner of war in Korea. His army buddies simply called him "the badest ass on the planet." Apparently his stepfather had twice tried to escape and was brought back to be severely beaten and tortured. His buddies were amazed that he survived.

He did not talk about those experiences but apparently they made him very bitter toward the world. His stepson began to feel some of his suppressed anger when he was five years old. The boy was at the dinner table anxiously waiting the dinner being served by his mother. As she served him some breaded tomatoes he remembers loudly telling her that he wasn't going to eat them.

His stepfather quietly stood up, took all of his food in his right hand and mashed it into his tiny face. From that time on he ate everything on his plate.

Those were the days when the old-time television sets often went on the blink. When they did a message would appear that read: "Please stand by ..."

Whenever this happened, Short Round's stepfather would make the boy stand stiffly at attention like a toy soldier beside the TV until the program they were watching came back on. Sometimes he stood there for two or three hours. He believes now that his stepfather was testing him as well as training him to be tough, to do what he was told to do even if he hated it.

And then there was the garage. The youngster called it The House of Pain where his stepfather would whip him when he thought the boy had done something that he disliked. He used a sturdy branch from a weeping willow tree.

He would pick the largest branches he could find and he would whip the boy across his bare back until the skin came off and he was bleeding. At the time the boy could only think of his stepfather as a monster.

Here's the way Short Round justified to himself his father's cruelty toward him:

"No matter how naughty I may have been or at least what he thought was being that way, how could a human-being do this to another, especially one so young? I just couldn't make sense of it. But you know, life has a way of protecting you from past pains. I survived, and in a way the discipline and the hardship he put me through taught me resilience, seriousness and confidence. I became a survivor because of it. Sometimes sad situations can bring about strength and lessons we sincerely needed to learn. This was one of those times."

He taught the small boy to fight hard against all bullies. If they were 20-pounds bigger than he was he should pick up a 20-pound club because in his words, "To make it fair you have to somehow excel and the club is the equalizer." He instilled in the boy the belief always that the bigger they were the harder they fell. Of course what he forgot to mention was that the bigger they were the harder they hit!

But over all as he looked back years later at what happened to him it wasn't just teaching him to be strong and able to stand up for himself without fear, it was also teaching him to be a soldier.

His stepfather was preparing him for the unknown, so that he could protect himself and be safe. The lesson the boy learned was that if he could make himself strong he would be safe.

Short Round believed that all of these lessons tried to make him strong, but at the same time these lessons probably made him eager to take risks that he shouldn't have taken to prove that he had what it took to be strong. He recognized this as a double-edged sword.

A part of his basic training in the service seemed extreme

and cruel but it too was intended to make him and his comrades stronger so that when extreme things happened in Vietnam, they would be better prepared to survive them.

This is what happened to him during basic training at Fort Polk, Louisiana. This basic training took place in a Louisiana mud swamp that even then had a bad reputation. I went through it in 1947 and wound up in the U.S. Army Ski Troops in the Italian Alps. But after that came preparation for us to become the spit and polish brigade assigned to garrison duty in Trieste. Our training involved cruelty beyond belief on an island off Venice. Initially it had been a stone barracks for Italian troops. As we marched in through the stone archway in the icy cold winter of '46 a hangman's noose dangled over our heads, welcoming us to what was then called the Lido Training Camp. The First Lieutenant that ran the facility with a cadre of musclemen said "You either graduate or go out of here in a box." Beatings by the cadre were common. After we graduated, both the commanding general and the lieutenant we called "Radar Ryan" were cashiered out of the army for things that happened at that training camp. *Time Magazine* told readers about it. Those of us who survived it couldn't have been happier.

Anyway, in those World War II years and after them the training facility in Louisiana was called Camp Polk. It was claimed in 1946 that Walter Winchell, who was a popular American newspaper and radio commentator, supposedly had a son who lost his life going through basic there. So, in one of his radio broadcasts, Winchell said, "If you have a son overseas, write to him. If you have a son at Camp Polk, Louisiana, pray for him." True or not, it was a miserable place that taught us how to soldier under the worse of conditions, and apparently by the time it was preparing soldiers for Vietnam it had added a few training embellishments.

Short Round said that when all of their basic training was over, there was one final wrap-up event which was directly related to where the men were going to be in combat. This was their final test before graduation:

At midnight Short Round's entire unit was taken to the furthest corners of Fort Polk's swampy wilderness. It was a moon-less night and no flashlights were allowed. Before the men was a mile of dense woodlands. They were told that they were to walk through that area and come out the other side without getting caught by an enemy force that would be hidden in the woods.

If you were caught and tapped you were to go with your captor without resisting. If you resisted you had to take the training program all over again. The men in his group saw it as a war game and they were gung-ho ready to take it on.

Everyone took off on a dead run through the black forest. But Short Round and his buddy took their time and walked. In the darkness they could hear the enemy catching their men and the guards saying, over and over, "You are caught," as they tapped out many of the runners.

To avoid being caught the two decided to climb a tree for safety. An hour later, when everything was quiet, they climbed down to the ground and walked quietly through the palmettos and trees again. A mile later they came out on a highway where their bus awaited them.

They were amazed to find that there were only two others like them that made it through the forest without being caught. So the four of them headed back to their barracks.

Abruptly at 6 a.m. they awakened to the sound of screaming sirens. They were told to go to a certain place for an assembly. It was an assembly all right; they were the only four people in the audience. Each one of their fellow comrades who had been caught was brought out one at a time. Almost every one of them had a large red swollen upper lip.

That's when they learned the rest of the story.

The prisoners that had been caught were placed in large metal drums with sealed lids. Inside they were subjected to loud pounding on the metal drums by their captors. They were then removed and told to lay flat on their backs. Each one of them was given the same torture treatment. To prevent them from lifting their head, a piano wire was stretched across their upper lip just under their nose a quarter inch away as their head was tilted back and water was forced down their nostrils with a syringe. If they struggled and raised their heads their upper lip got bruised by the tight piano wire.

While this was occurring their captors fired questions at them, asking their rank, name and serial number which of course they gave freely. But there were also questions about their families and their personal life, details that they alone knew. Bottom line – *Every one of those men gave in and talked!*

Short Round couldn't believe it. He couldn't believe that so many gave in. Here he had been tortured all of his life and he was damn sure not going to give in. He almost wished he had been caught so that he could prove it to the captors.

Three days later they graduated from Fort Polk and were on their way to Vietnam.

5

One More for Short Round

Short Round turned out to be one of the best Tunnel Rats they ever had. He and the Old Man's adopted company watchdog "Lifer" became heroes to everyone who knew how well they took out the enemy in the tunnels. These were described in *Tunnel Tales*.

Things had been unusually quiet for the company but that changed one-day when Short Round saw two new guys come into their compound. They reported to the Top Sergeant and ten minutes later the Third Platoon was told to gear up. As if it was an afterthought, the Top casually said, "You better go along with them on this one, Short- Round. Leave Lifer but take your .45 and nothing else."

Short Round knew what that meant. They had found tunnels. Since he was their only tunnel rat he got to do the dirty work.

When they got to the area he saw that they had uncovered a couple of spider holes. Everyone approached them quietly. They didn't want to alert any of the enemy that might be hunkered down in the dark there. Usually these places were short sniper hides but that wasn't the case with these.

In the past they might just have tossed in a couple grenades and closed shop on them. But command now wanted any tunnels they found checked out. We were learning that there was more to some of those places than just a sniper hide.

With his .45 going first, Short Round eased himself down into the first hole, and crawled carefully head-first along its narrow shaft, using his elbows and knees to move himself along but slowly as his left hand felt the floor of the tunnel in front of him. He left his small pocket light in his right hand breast pocket. No sense making himself a lighted target right off the bat. Instead, every few moments he paused, listening intently as his eyes adjusted to the total darkness surrounding him.

As usual he was ramped up for what was ahead. He heard his heart beating rapidly and a band of sweat popped out on his forehead. Like a blind man his fingers were now his eyes in the dark moving slowly back and forth in front of him, his fingertips lightly touching the roughness in front of him.

No spider-webs told him this was not an old, abandoned tunnel. Everything in front of him was smooth and clean. Someone had been there recently.

As his eyes finally adapted to the dark, he squirmed forward. His movement, plus the sound of his clothing against the rough ground rasped loudly in his ears. Everything was punctuated by his heavy breathing. He fought to get control of it; to calm it. He was suffering from new tunnel excitement. He soon would get it all under control.

In the abrupt silence when he stopped, he thought he could hear a kind of sing-song noise. It sounded far off. He tried to identify what it was.

He held his breath and followed his left hand moving back and forth in front of him as though it was fingering keys on an invisible piano. But his touch was a lot softer because all it took to trigger a thin copper trip wire was the slightest pressure. That's all a buried Coke can grenade needed to move an already half-pulled pin the fraction of an inch that dropped the spoon and after that he wouldn't have time to even know what happened.

Suddenly the sing-song sound in the distance stopped. He heard what sounded like a distant muffled cough. His roving fingers felt nothing on his right side. He paused and let them do the looking for him, like a blind man touching things and then seeing them all in his mind.

Like a five-legged spider Short Round's left hand found no wall to his right. The shaft turned abruptly in that direction. Sweat was running down and burning his eyes.

He had expected an abrupt turn one way or the other. He figured he knew why too. That sharp turn back on itself immediately provided a hide for anyone in the tunnel ahead of him. If he had used his light it would have fooled him into thinking the tunnel continued on straight and there was no one there. But an armed VC in black pajamas would not only be invisible but he could pop out and shoot or stab him instantly.

That's why Short Round was using all of his other senses, "feeling" and "sensing" almost unconsciously, what might be threatening in the darkness ahead. If there had been someone waiting around that corner, he knew one thing from experience – he would have been alerted early by the smell of his fishy stink. That was what the company's mascot, Lifer, alerted them to whenever the Vietnamese were near enough to smell. He bristled and growled because he picked up on their scent much sooner than the men did.

In the darkness at the bend in the tunnel, Short Round grinned to himself. He was getting almost as good as Lifer sniffing them. His nose told him no one was waiting in the darkness around that corner.

As he carefully squeezed himself around that abrupt turn, he thought how clever it was that it was there. It could do a lot more than hide an assailant. Almost every tunnel had it. It was there to protect anyone down there from a grenade explosion near the entrance.

Now, his heart quickened at what he saw down the new shaft in the distance. He saw the pale yellow glow of lantern light. Someone coughed again. That sing-song sound was someone talking in Vietnamese. He was either talking to himself or to someone.

Short Round went into his Inch-Worm mode, low and

slow, inching himself along with his elbows, knees and boot tips with the .45 pointing straight ahead aimed at that faint light.

He was in control of himself now. His heart had slowed to its normal controlled but calmly excited rate, his breathing was silent, as he sipped short breaths in and out quietly; and the shake had gone from his hands. Even his sweating had stopped. Now all he felt was the high of being in full control of himself but ready for intense action. He lived for that feeling. It was exhilarating. He rode his adrenaline high with deep satisfaction knowing that it was his reward for this kind of life. It prepared him for what was about to come. It hyped him up for what he had to do, and would do expertly, like he always did. He was a professional, at the top of his game. He was looked up to and respected. He knew that now he had it made in the shade and he was enjoying every moment of it.

As he inched closer to the two men sitting with the lantern between them totally engrossed in what they were talking about, Short Round stopped, aimed and his forefinger tightened on the curved trigger of his Colt .45.

The sudden explosion of sound in that tiny tunnel completely blew out his hearing and left him with nothing but a white sound roar. One of the VC slumped, dead. The other leaped up and bolted as Short Round fired twice more. But he missed as the man disappeared into the darkness.

Short Round had no intention of going after him. He put himself in reverse and as swiftly as he could he elbowed and toed his way back out of there. He sweated profusely now, his heart hammered and his high had disappeared.

His buddies helped drag him back out of the tight entranceway. Everyone listened eagerly as Short Round described what had happened. No one cared to go after the one that got away. He was long gone from there by now.

The guys got busy with C4 to collapse that tunnel, leaving the others alone until they could be checked out another day. Then everyone hurried back to camp. Mission accomplished.

6

The Wannabe

After chow that night, a recent replacement, a skinny young guy with a baby face who Short Round didn't know, cornered him and wanted to go along with him on one of his tunnel clearing trips just to see how Short Round did it.

Short Round looked him up and down and noted that he had the build for it, but he didn't think he would last long being a tunnel rat. So he intentionally tried to talk the kid out of it.

But the youngster was adamant and the more Short Round tried to dissuade him the more the kid insisted that he could make a good tunnel rat.

"Why should you get all the glory?" the kid asked.

Short Round grinned and slowly shook his head. "Buddy, there's no glory in what you have to do down there. There's no glory at all. All you have to be is stupid."

"Yeah, sure," the kid said. "I still wanna go down and do it."

Top, who had heard the exchange and had already been approached several times by the soldier wanting to learn how to be a tunnel rat, finally shrugged and said, "Okay, kid. If he'll take you."

Deep down inside Short Round knew that he should have someone trained to take his place just in case something happened to him. Nobody else in the outfit was built for it. This kid had the build, but did he have the guts? Short Round had let one of the enemy escape … one that might be waiting for him in one of the tunnels next time. He began to get concerned about his own mortality. At the same time if he could save one kid from getting into this crazy suicidal crap he was determined to keep trying.

But the skinny guy kept insisting stubbornly that no matter how Short Round felt about it he wanted to be allowed to go into a tunnel on his own the next morning. Thinking how foolish that was, Short Round knew that nothing else would change the kid's mind until he got a taste of it himself. He remembered his own obsession with it so he half understood where the kid was coming from.

The short tunnel rat knew that sooner or later he had to turn it over to someone else before he ran out of luck. Sooner or later it was bound to happen.

After chow Top talked to Short Round saying that the kid sounded as crazy as Short Round about those tunnels. But he decided to let him go if he wanted to try it.

So Short Round and the Top told the kid they were going to let him go in a tunnel by himself the next morning to see what it was like. Sad but true, thought Short Round.

But maybe this was the wrong time because the whole outfit was on edge knowing that a lot of Viet Cong were in the area. They figured many of the enemy hid in the tunnels to avoid being discovered. If anything brought them out ready for a firefight it was the dark of night.

So before dark, just in case, rather than wait around for an attack, the Americans doubled the number of Claymore mines and trip flares they put out around their perimeter. That night Short Round along with his buddies, Oreo and Bill all pulled guard duty together.

It seemed to them that they had barely got into their fox holes when Lifer started her all too familiar growl. Since their little adopted dog had never let them down when she sensed the enemy in the area, everyone was on the alert, expecting something to happen.

Short Round dropped his hand down to her. He felt her back fur standing up, and she was trembling. He quickly climbed out of his fox hole to alert his buddy, Indy, in the hooch.

"Hey, buddy, get up. Lifer sez they're out there!"

Without a word the soldier bounced off his cot and hurried toward the First Platoon. Before Short Round made it back to his foxhole the night sky lit up with illumination rounds from their own mortars.

The men looked out into the flickering bright light that bathed their perimeter defenses and were stunned by what they saw. The VC were out there alright looking weirder than anyone had ever seen them before. Two lines of them were flat on the ground head to feet, head to feet, crawling under their defenses, *on their backs!*

Crawling uphill … two lines of them like a pair of giant caterpillars! When they reached the company's illumination trip wires they touched the wires lightly with the palms of their hands and tapped the soldier below them with their foot. It was crazy, but they knew exactly what they were doing and how to make it through the company's defenses. There were about 20 or 30 of the enemy out there doing that kind of stuff and man did Short Round and his buddies ever light them up in a hurry with everything they had!

It was bedlam; everyone firing at once. The noise was deafening. Explosions, smoke, screaming, rapid firing. Many of the guys had put a tracer round in for every fifth bullet and these were streaking red all over the place. It was the Forth of July with horizontal rockets. The outfit's machine-gunners joined everyone else, raking them back and forth. Then the mortar platoon started dropping rapid-fire rounds into that bunch of bad guys. It was a massacre!

But weirdly, the next morning when the American's made their body count all they found were 8 bodies! Where the devil were the rest of them? It baffled everyone. Some may have escaped, but most of the guys guessed that somehow after the firing stopped, the enemy had stolen back in to recover their bodies. (Later it was learned that the enemy dead often ended up in mass graves in the tunnels. In other cases they just ended up in side chambers stacked high and rotting.)

Despite all this action none of it dampened the eagerness of the skinny wannabe. He was more anxious than ever a couple days later to get into one of those tunnels. Short Round and the Top both tried to talk him out of it one last time. But it was useless. Too many of those tempting tunnels were out there and he had made up his mind.

So Short Round took the fellow's weapon, backpack and his dog-tags. Then he gave him his .45 and his flashlight.

The newbie was beside himself he was so excited. He could hardly wait to crawl down into one of the tunnels they had found not far from the one where they had lost the VC the day before. The last they saw of him were his feet wiggling as he disappeared into the tunnel's small black hole.

The rest of the guys hung around the opening to that rabbit hole straining to hear anything that would tell them what was happening underground.

They waited and they sweated. Nobody talked as they strained to listen. About ten minutes later they heard muffled gunfire. But it was from an AK-47. Not Short Round's .45.

The guys were shocked; especially Short Round. He blamed himself for letting that stubborn baby-faced kid talk him into it. He felt he had just let someone commit suicide.

The men where trying to decide what to do. Short Round geared up to go recover his body. Suddenly the guy popped out of the tunnel, shaking uncontrollably with his left hand bleeding profusely from a gunshot wound. The medic jumped forward to give him first aid.

He said he had dropped Short Round's flashlight when he got shot. Then he told them that the guy that shot him took off and disappeared in the tunnel. They wondered how many more were down there.

Short Round saw Top looking at him with a question on his face. He knew what that meant. Short Round nodded and said, "Let's go get him, but not in *this* tunnel."

The wannabe tunnel rat who got shot on his first tunnel rat operation was wide-eyed and confused. Scared out of his wits he babbled over and over, "Man, you guys are nuts ... completely nuts. I'll never ever do that damn thing again. That's crazy shit!"

"That's what I tried to tell you," said Short Round quietly. "Only crazies go into tunnels. Somebody upstairs must like you. You got a million dollar wound that's going to take you home for good. Buddy, you sure lucked out!"

Short Round was trying to sound sarcastic but he did it mostly to keep his mind off what he had to do now. He had to go down that hole and find the guy. That kind of stuff was going to take him out sooner or later. When it happened let the rest of them worry about who his replacement would be. He was totally pissed at himself for letting the kid go in because he was not at all ready for it. Short Round knew he should have at least told him to keep the damn flashlight off. But he hadn't. He especially felt bad about that. At least the kid survived. He got enough of a taste to know he never wanted to go there again.

Before Short Round pocketed his backup flashlight to go down into another tunnel however, the tough little tunnel rat wanted to be sure nothing crazy had happened to his .45. He took several minutes to dismantle the weapon and put it back together again ... like he always did after someone else had used his weapon.

When he finally decided on which hole he was going to crawl into he hesitated. For the first time he felt fear, knowing that somewhere down there the enemy knew he was coming and would be ready to deal with him. As he squirmed his way into the tight enclosure Short Round felt worse than he ever felt before.

He took out his backup light and did what he always did. Once he got into the main tunnel he turned it on about three seconds to get his bearings, then he turned it off while he carefully crawled along the tunnel feeling everything in front of him for the next few minutes. He disliked the idea that for some days now the enemy below knew he and his men were exploring the tunnels. What surprises were they setting for him?

This long-admired little tunnel rat was destined to have such a near death experience in this tunnel that he told Top it was his last. As described in my earlier book, Top wondered why it had taken him so long to make that decision.

Not long after that Short Round went home, married and enjoyed life to its fullest. So did the wannabe who bragged that once upon a time in Vietnam he had been a Tunnel Rat.

7

Secrets of the VC's Underground World

Here's what the Viet Cong planned to achieve with their tunnels. In a sense, the VC's reason for the extensive tunneling system in their country was basically as air raid shelters built for the same reason they were built in Europe during WW2. But these were intended to include much more than just a shelter. Here's a translation of what a primary Viet Cong secret publication explained to their people on this subject:

"(The tunnels') main purpose for sheltering is only significant when they serve our soldiers in combat activities. As shelters their great advantages are wasted. Their construction should therefore be in accordance with the combat plan as drafted by the villages and hamlets. There should be combat posts in our tunnels for providing continuous support to our troops even when the enemy occupies our villages. Our armed forces must be able to enter one passageway into the tunnels and exit from another, or disappear and appear suddenly in order to attack the enemy."

They were told to expect the possibility of fighting from inside the underground tunnels. They said, "A secret passage must be available from which our troops may escape and fight in the open, or re-enter the underground tunnels if necessary."

They were told that the tunnel reduced the enemy's superior firepower by helping their forces launch close-in attacks on the enemy along with the opportunity to seize their weapons. They enabled the Viet Cong to wear down the enemy's potential with relatively few weapons at their disposal. The tunnels also provided more mobility for the enemy troops who could then move safely without fear of aerial bombardments or their encountering enemy patrols.

One of them pointed out that it enabled them, the Viet Cong, to fight from different hidden positions. They were told that because the activities of the military and the guerrillas required them to appear and disappear quickly, the entrances to these underground systems should be located like the corners of a triangle so that each could support the other in combat. The troops must be able to retreat from an underground tunnel through a secret opening so that they may continue to fight.

The tunnel builders were warned not to build their tunnel within 1.5 meters of the surface. The deeper the better to avoid damage from the vibration of explosions. Also, it is interesting to note, that they were very aware of monsoon rains entering their system and flooding them out. To counter that, about every 30 meters they were told to dig deep sumps for the runoff. The ideal distances between entrances should be 40 or 50 meters, but in some cases it could be 20 to 30 meters.

There were also tunnels built for both upper and lower class individuals. These tunnels were built by the individuals themselves. The lower class tunnels were not fortified as well as those for the upper classes. (This was probably because the upper classes hired lower class citizens to dig for them but with *their* specifications.)

Even the kind of accommodations varied in different tunnels. Most of the tunnels were strong enough to withstand elements of the destructive warfare brought on by the American troops.

As for the Americans, this idea of the enemy living and fighting from underground tunnels was an unexpected nightmare. Totally frustrated, our military officers had no idea how to deal with these odd circumstances. It seemed that the enemy had everything going for them. It was a clever defense.

No one knew the extent of this unique defense system. The enemy could pop up anywhere and fight, then disappear into this labyrinth where they were completely protected. They could travel long distances underground, then unexpectedly re-emerge to fight again, before once more disappearing underground.

If they were wounded, they were taken down into the tunnels and given treatment. If there was a top-side firefight and some of their comrades were killed, if possible the bodies were not left behind but disappeared into the tunnels for burial.

The interesting thing as we learned more about these tunnels was that they were all dug by hand. Most of them were begun many years before our Vietnam War. Once begun, it continued and never stopped. Initially the people were given a booklet of information, which translated said:

"These passages are dug in the following way: with digging devices and with the hands called manual digging. These are dug usually by two persons who rotate in digging and shoveling the earth. They used a primitive earth removal device that stood over the holes during the digging. It enabled the removal of the dirt, but how it was deposed of was another matter; a most important one."

One of the officers in charge of tunnel digging during the war said that he had spent five years on a tunnel digging assignment. His eyes, from being in the dark such a long time, became so sensitized to daylight that today he wears heavy sunglasses to be able to tolerate the average sunlight.

The average excavation at that time was described as about a cubic meter per person per day. Think of that. In truth it was reported that the average excavation was more like half of that, but it was also noted that if workers were working near a ventilation hole where they got better air, this would speed up production and they moved more earth. To appreciate this momentous effort by everyone those tunnels extended for miles! In the Cu Chi area near Saigon they comprised an underground web that extended up to 75 miles early in the war. By war's end this distance had doubled. Unknowingly, the American Army built a huge military base on top of all those tunnels. We soon wondered how they attacked us at night in that base wherever they wanted and then totally disappeared. They used typical guerrilla hit and run tactics. But for some time we wondered how they did it and where they disappeared to.

Apparently everybody in the country, early on, was involved in this program, the men, the women, the old, the young and the children. In *Tunnel Tales* I described how they would sink several vertical holes and then dig horizontally to link them up as one continual horizontal tunnel. This was generally the procedure.

After the war a Saigon citizen was interviewed who was described as a medium sized male with gray hair, scrawny arms, tired looking eyes behind thick lens glasses. He said that in 1962 when he was much more physically fit he worked with the Viet Cong in the country. He said that for him and many others digging tunnels was their everyday job because they lived in the tunnels. He said he had to have two or three spare tunnels in case the enemy destroyed one in a bombing raid. He always needed to have a back-up tunnel to go to so he dug every day of his life.

The soil in the area where he was digging was a mixture of sand and soil. In the rainy season he said it was soft like sugar. In the dry time it was hard as rock. The man said that at such a time, if he managed to dig down 30 centimeters (less than a foot) a day in six hours, it was a huge achievement. Of course it was much easier to dig in the rainy season. He said his digging tools were a hoe as small as a saucer and he had to kneel or sit down on the ground. He said he had to find hard soil which he could always find at the base of a bamboo tree or wherever there was a termite nest. That soil could stand the weight of a tank. He and others would dig in teams of three. One digging the soil, the second one removing it from the area and the third one pulling it to the surface.

You wonder how people got rid of all of that freshly dug soil. Somehow it had to disappear. During the war their methods were often ingenious. When the aerial bombardments began it was easy to use the craters as dumpsites.

The authors of the tunnel booklet also noted that removed tunnel soil could also be made into basements for houses, or used in furrows for growing potatoes, or combat trenches, as well as poured into streams. But it was never to be left heaped up beside tunnel entrances. They emphasized that everything had to be done to conceal the underground tunnel from the enemy's eyes. And amazingly it was.

Our average soldiers might not notice some of these details, but the Viet Cong felt entirely different about the Green Berets. They learned that they had been trained to look for the slightest kind of telltale evidence that would indicate a freshly dug tunnel. The average foot soldier could care less. An enemy who lived, fought, hid, and appeared or disappeared underground he not only hadn't heard about, but he had never had any training on how to fight that kind of war before. That fact took a heavy toll on our troops.

8

Learning from the Enemy

What we learned from captured enemy prisoners told us many things about these tunnels. A Viet Cong guerilla named Ngo Gan Gaing, was captured by the South Vietnamese and information he provided became part of a sixteen page debriefing document on tunnels. It told captors that "Whenever a tunnel was used as an open bunker, the tunnel builders gave it a special roof. It was constructed by using a layer of 50 centimeter bamboo poles followed by a layer of 50mm husks, this was followed by a layer of dirt and on top of the dirt they planted flowers or used fallen trees as camouflage."

It is hard to believe, but the prisoner swore that if a 200-kilogram bomb fell 30 meters from a tunnel there would be no damage. Supposedly, the leaves and the husks used were excellent protection against bomb blasts. The bamboo poles were used because they were resilient. The prisoner said that in April 1966 a plane dropped a 200 kg bomb that hit right on this kind of tunnel. The dirt and husks caved in, but the soldiers that were hiding inside were not wounded.

We all know now that some of the tunnels were mined for enemy intruders. You wonder how they kept from getting caught up in their own booby traps. One of our more experienced tunnel rats was guided by what kind of evidence he found to indicate just how heavily used different tunnels were. Abandoned tunnels could be expected to be booby-trapped. Here's how he knew the difference.

"I look closely at the entrance of a newly opened tunnel.

When I see hundreds of tiny glittering spider eyes looking back at me I figure that's an abandoned tunnel and it probably has mines. If those glittering eyes are all around the outside but not in the middle, that tunnel is used occasionally and may not be mined."

But if there are no spider eyes that tunnel is used and there may be someone hiding down there waiting for you. Some tunnel rats used trained dogs to sniff out a tunnel before they went down into it. It is reported that some of the dogs came back with bloodied jaws.

Here is what the VC told their people about setting mines: They should set the mines and traps but were not to arm them with the trip wire. They said that the soldiers inside should be able to move to side passages or other levels before the trip wires were set.

An enemy document captured late in the war described the enemy's tunnels in detail. It said that the tunnels were dug in such a way that it enabled the villages and hamlets to become fortresses. Even though the enemy might be several times superior to them in strength and weapons, they would not be chased from the battlefield because they could launch surprise attacks from their underground tunnels.

It went on to say that the tunnels were critical for launching close-in attacks on the Americans and it gave the enemy an opportunity to seize their weapons and could provide the Viet Cong with excellent mobility and as the unlucky 25th Infantry Division was to discover "We may attack the enemy right in the center of his formations or keep on fighting from different places."

Another feature that we didn't know about was that as increasingly larger bombs were being used against them, threatening their tunnel system, the Vietnamese dug A-shaped underground rooms designed to stand up against an artillery barrage or bomb blasts. Another interesting feature, that we never learned until much later, was that this cone-shaped room acted as an underground amplifier of sound so that they could hear B-52 bombers approaching their area long before they got there. This was really the only warning system they had for those living in the tunnels that an attack might be coming their way.

They were well aware that as long as they could keep the entrances secret, the enemy was less likely to be invading their tunnel system. The way they hid these entrances was extremely clever. If the small trap door entrance was covered with leaves, for example, they never let them change color indicating they were dead because they knew that Special Forces Green berets were trained to look for these things as indicators of a tunnel entrance. So they religiously got rid of these telltale leaves and replaced them with live green ones, even to the extent of maintaining live grasses and plants on the covers to the entrances.

It was important to put an entryway someplace where Americans would never think to look for one. Clever enemy minds quickly found such places. Under cooking fires was one common place. Or in a pigpen so stinking and noxious no soldier would ever think of looking there. Other unlikely places were a corner post of a building, or an animal shelter under a roof and animals.

One captured Viet Cong officer after the war said that they had special workshops in the tunnels where they worked on American ordinance that had not exploded. They tried to keep track of where they all landed. They dug them up, dismantled them in their tunnels; and then fitted them with their own detonators. Once recharged, the shells were set off with batteries or rigged as booby traps. They claimed to also have found a large number of claymore mines that had not exploded for some reason or another. Often the VC officer said they had more of these mines than they could use.

Coca-Cola cans we provided them with turned into hand grenades that the Viet Cong made lethal and threw back at the American troops. All of these aluminum cans were used by workers in their underground workshops. They loaded the Coke Cans with bomb fragments, then TNT was poured into the middle and a homemade detonator was placed on top.

Many of these tunnel systems had workmen who just made and repaired firearms all the time. In all cases where electrical power was required underground to run these workshops, most of it was done with small hand or foot generators. In some cases, a small gasoline driven generator was used, but these were rare. Usually they were pedal generators, some hand generators from China, and of course batteries. Often they managed to steal our batteries which they used.

As early as 1963 the ARVN [**Army of the Republic of Viet-Nam**. ARVN (pronounced "Arvin") was South Vietnam's army. During the war, ARVN troops were advised by American officers and fought alongside American soldiers. Also referred to as "Marvin the ARVN."] This South Vietnamese Army which was then fighting a losing war against Viet Cong forces had warned the American Advisors about the tunnels and how well they were hidden. At one time they were told that they often occurred in Vietnamese cemeteries and if you carried a long pointed stick, you could shove them into the graves. If they hit the top of a coffin you were all right but if you hit nothing it might be the opening to a Viet Cong tunnel.

Interestingly, none of the ARVN officers or soldiers ever ventured down into any of the tunnels to explore them or to have a shoot-out with the Viet Cong. This is something their officers just never considered. Not only that, but they often concealed tunnel openings they found to avoid someone suggesting they climb down into them and confront the enemy. These were our allies, our local militia trained to fight against the North Vietnamese Army, or so we thought!

The only tactic they seemed set on using was to surround an enemy tunnel entrance and wait for the guerillas to come out. So it's not surprising that by the time the American Army arrived in 1965 the Viet Cong were well established in their underground network of bunkers, work shops, hospitals and storage tunnels. They were well prepared for a long siege.

9

Aussie Tunnel Rats

Nam 1967

It takes real guts to be the first one going headfirst down a small black hole in enemy country that hugs you so tight you either go in with your hands in front or they will never get there to wipe those strong spider-webs off your face. So tight it's like screwing your body into the clammy ground with no intention of coming back out because you don't know how to crawl uphill backwards. You're not even sure you will ever get back to daylight if something leaps out of that superheated foul fetid blackness ahead of you and with searing pain snuffs out your life right then and there. Then the overwhelming relief when in fact it doesn't happen, but you take it out on yourself by silently yelling, *"Damnit heart, stop hammering so frickin' hard!"*

In his book *TUNNEL RATS The larrikin Aussie legends who discovered the Viet Cong's secret weapon,* authors Jimmy Thomson with Sandy MacGregor, pull no punches as they open their book with this visceral version of every new tunnel rat's feelings as they make that first venture into that living nightmare. Here's how they describe it from the Australian point of view:

> You launch yourself headfirst down a hole in the
> ground that's scarcely wide enough for your shoulders.
> After a couple of meters of slipping and wriggling straight

down, the narrow tunnel takes a U-turn towards the surface, then twists again before heading off further than you can see with the battery-powered lamp attached to your cap. Because the tunnel has recently been full of smoke and tear gas, you are wearing a gasmask. The eyepieces steam up and the sound of your own breathing competes with the thump of your heart to deafen you. You know you are not safe. You are in your enemy's domain and one of your comrades— a friend— has already died in a hole in the ground just like this one. This is the stuff of nightmares: a tunnel that's almost too small to crawl along dug by and for slightly built and wiry Vietnamese, not broad-backed Aussies or Americans. Every inch forward has to be checked for booby traps, so you have a bayonet in one hand. Every corner could conceal an enemy soldier, perhaps one who can retreat no further, so you have a pistol in the other. There's no room to turn around. Going forward is difficult enough; backing out is nigh impossible. You know that the enemy knows you're there. You know your miner's light makes a perfect target. You switch it off. The silence is ominous, though not quite complete as the pounding of your heart throbs through your body. The velvet darkness is all-engulfing. Then it becomes harder to catch your breath. You become light-headed, then dizzy and confused as the air runs out. Reason and sense evaporate as the darkness claims you. But you get a grip ... you breathe ... you bring it all back under control because the alternative— blind panic— means death. And you move on. That's how it felt to be a Tunnel Rat.

Most of the Aussie troops had heard about the tunnels of Vietnam but no one had much information about them. Then one day the captain and his 3 Field Group found some and they wondered how to handle the situation. The first thing the captain did was come up and look at the small opening; then he said, "Well, boys, what do we do now?"

They had no idea what to expect or what to do. But the captain knew that he wanted to find out what was down there. He had no intention of ordering one of his men into the tunnel because no one knew what might happen. So he decided to inspect it himself. He said,

"Just in case you boys need to haul me out fast I got one of the blokes to tie a rope around my ankles. Then they lowered me head first into the hole with a torch (flashlight) in one hand and a bayonet in the other.

"I was let down the tunnel with a guy after me and I didn't know what to expect."

All he did was shine his light in front of him to see if he could find anything. He said he realized it didn't matter how small a tunnel it was, you never knew when it was going to turn around a bend and you didn't know what was there or what might be in the floor. You didn't know if it was abandoned or booby-trapped and you sure didn't know where it was going. In other words, it was scary.

The tunnel that he was first exploring ended less than 30 meters away under a house that had already been cleared. It had not been inhabited by the Viet Cong so he didn't think there was anything sinister about it.

As his group began searching the various tunnels they found that most of them ended up under a house. Entering them from one of the local grass huts called a hooch, they came out in a storm drain or a nearby rice paddy. That suggested that these might be escape tunnels; someplace where the inhabitants could make their get-away if their hooch was being attacked. A backdoor they alone knew about.

The captain had his men go through his tunnel one by one to see what it was like for their selves. Later they found another tunnel entrance down a well. After that they realized that there was a network of open trenches in the area that ran into tunnels; some of which had small room off of the main tunnel. From that they figured the tunnels were either for personal protection or were escape routes. The captain's men found that most of them were not booby-trapped and some were not even hidden, but were simply open.

The troop's unofficial photographer snapped a picture of the captain's boots protruding from the tunnel with the rope around his ankles. After the picture was sent back to Australia, where it appeared in a weekly magazine, the military quickly sent off a letter to the captain saying that they were horrified to see a picture of the troop commander going down into tunnels. The captain received a polite reprimand and a firm order from the Brigadier Commander in Saigon telling the officer that tunnel clearance was not a job for captains and that he was to stay above ground. This was the standing order throughout the Allies in Nam that officers were not to enter tunnels.

During Operation Crimp both the Americans and the Aussies were assigned areas near Cu Chi to search out and destroy these tunnels, mainly because we suspected the enemy was hiding out in them by day, and attacking from them at night. Oddly this area was heavily laced with tunnels. Only many years latter would the Allies learn why.

One such group of tunnel rats, eager to learn all they could about these tunnels, worked with Aussie engineers exploring the diversities of rooms and tunnels mainly used for storage of weapons and materials. In one tragic case they had a large tunnel rat who pushed his way down into a narrow tunnel that dead-ended. And because of his size he was unable to back out. He blacked out. As others frantically tried to dig down to him by the time they reached him it was too late. He had suffocated.

The common practice was to use a Mighty Mite air blower that blasted fresh air down into these shafts that they were exploring. They also tried to keep track of the tunnel rat as he moved horizontally through these intricate underground passages by equipping them with radio telephones so topside troops could try to pinpoint their locations from the surface. If they then got in trouble they could quickly dig down and recover them. The difficulty in many cases was that the shafts were so small that the tunnel rats ran out of air very easily and got into trouble before they could be rescued.

One soldier said, he was tail-end Charlie sitting in the

dark with no torch (light), no phone or anything when the guys he was working with were ahead of him. The two men there suddenly got very quiet. He reported this to his superiors, who were going to send in a rescue team, when he said I know exactly where they are, so he said, "I shot down there and there's the first one named Tommy just sitting and giggling and chuckling and carrying on. I thought he was pissed. I really did. I thought he had found a rice wine stash or some bloody thing. Then I realized he was gassed. So I grabbed him by the scruff of his neck and dragged him the 50 or 60 meters back and stuck him out through the hole."

He went back and dragged out the other one too. By the next day both were all right, having apparently been deprived of oxygen to the point where they were about to pass out.

In one of the tunnels the Aussies found that it had been set up with secret triggers to hand grenades in trees outside so that if you tried to remove the cover to the tunnel the exploding grenades took you out.

In one instance one of the Aussie tunnel rats managed to step into a hidden pocket that put a sharpened punji stake through his foot. But those types of traps were rare in the underground tunnels. If the enemy was determined to plant some kind of trap it usually had to do with structure such as a trapdoor or an exit that might be booby trapped with a grenade in a Coke can, its pin almost out and a hidden copper wire that required a slight depression before detonation.

Other tunnels proved completely free of booby traps. The reason for this is that the tunnels in this area were intended to be used for equipment storage and weapons that had to be visited frequently by the Viet Cong. So they didn't mess them up with booby traps. Some were found, but they weren't primed to go. Their pins were in the grenades but un-pulled. But if a fleeing enemy was being pursued and knew where that trap was, he could set it in a jiffy.

Some of the tunnels were death traps on their own. Without adequate ventilation, the stagnant air and the general lack of oxygen was a deadly combination. Many of the Aussies who spent hours underground exploring these places wore cumbersome gas masks. These were useless where there was little oxygen. They wore them because troops earlier had pumped smoke and tear gas into these places hoping to flush out the VC who might be lurking in that steamy darkness.

Both the residual smoke and gas permeated those hot, clammy walls and the tunnel reeked of the stuff long after the first troops were there. Complaints later were that the gas caused skin irritation that bothered the exploring rats and they made many first aid visits due to it. These determined tunnel hunters learned to keep what they called a Mighty Mite air blower working behind them that pumped some semblance of fresh air into the places where they blindly fumbled around. The units saw plenty of action pumping what air they could down into these endless catacombs so the tunnel rats could get the job done of securing them.

They also introduced dogs to route out any of the enemy before the men exposed themselves to danger. The dogs were trained to attack any person found there smelling of stinking dried fish. Anyone else who smelled otherwise was probably considered pretty stinky to the vicious attack dog, but at least he was doggy friendly, earning him a lick in the face rather than a bite on the snout.

Encountering a dog in a tunnel without expecting it had to be exciting. As one rat described it the first time he encountered one of these prowling, snarling attack dogs in the darkness from another group of rats, it was quite an anus-puckering experience for him.

That night he said he could hear the sound of the Viet Cong apparently trying to dig themselves out. The Aussies tried to dig down to them and the entrances were opened and gas was pumped in to flush them out. But no one came out. Apparently they made their way to another escape tunnel.

Despite the threat of bad air and the possibility of getting themselves in a situation where they might not come out of it, this Australian outfit had no problem with the hazards. They were all keen to go down into the tunnels because of what they might find in terms of war prizes. One of their members ended up with a nice Czech sniper's rifle. It came about as he chased a wounded Cong into a tunnel. Apparently the infantry had shot him on the surface and he dived down into this tunnel and was getting away.

One of the pursuers said, after they got down there and was chasing him, he could hear him in front. This rat was wearing one of their helmet lights powered by dry-cell batteries, but he didn't switch it on for fear he would become a target. He then mentions something interesting. He mentioned seeing what he called "phosphorous markings in the dark."

This is the first time my research ever found mention of them being used in tunnels. We now know these had been placed there by the Viet Cong so that they could follow the luminous patches inside the tunnels without requiring lights. They put the markers at the corners of the tunnels where they knew what to expect. These Aussie tunnel rats wore lights but they never used them for obvious reasons. They only switched them on when they had to … when they came to a trapdoor or a dead end. Or something they really wanted to see.

This phosphorous material, that the Aussies described, was often used by the Vietnamese when it was too dangerous to turn on a light. It was made from crushed fireflies mixed with a waxy plant substance. The enemy often used it quite cleverly on the backpacks of carriers hiking along the Ho Chi Minh Trail at night. All they had to do was follow that luminous green palm-sized spot on the man ahead of them as they brought in supplies for their troops in South Vietnam. During jungle warfare during World War II, Japanese officers used the same kind of luminous substance on the palms of their hands to read maps at night.

The rat who was pursuing the wounded sniper said, "Anyway, I never actually saw him but I could hear him and he wasn't all that far in front of me. Eventually I came to the rifle he had dropped, probably because it was too cumbersome and slowing him down. It was in a leather case and I thought, 'What do I do? Take this prize or chase him? I knew some bastard would come behind me and grab it. So I said, fuck it. I didn't have any communications back to the surface or anything, so I just dragged it back. I got out and I said, 'He got away but I got this.'

"And the grunts were okay about it. They said a trophy was better than a kill any day."

One of his other comrades got a different surprise. When he turned the corner in a tunnel he came face to face with a pair of piercing eyes. "It was one of the better frights of my life," he said. "Picture this … a six foot drop down the tunnel, a seventy foot crawl along it and I might add blood at the entrance. Right turn, left turn, upper part ended in a hut. When I got out I went into another hut that had a concealed room under it. It was a storeroom full of 81mm mortars, guns and ammo. This helped fill out our own explosives. I took a couple of the mortars to be used in demolition of the other tunnel.

"We went back to the previous tunnel, this time down, down, down and I crawled in with the 81mm mortars. I didn't have enough hands.

"I started around a corner and all I saw were two eyes looking at me. I ducked back. In the dark with my mind racing, my first thought was, *Jesus! There's a Viet Cong around the corner!*

"When I stopped shaking I put the pistol around the corner followed by the torch. Then I realized that the eyes belonged to a big dog that was growling at me …" He recognized it as one of his buddies' fish-sniffing attack dogs.

As soon as the dog got a whiff of the scared rat it stopped growling; started whining and swiftly crawled up to lick him all over his face. [Probably relieved to find a buddy.] The disadvantaged but happy grunt couldn't back-crawl fast enough to avoid that warm, wet slobbery tongue. But boy, was he relieved it wasn't a Viet Cong!

The Aussies didn't have an easy time of it. They kept running into trapdoors or booby traps every 20 meters or so. On top of that they were burning their hands and necks from the tear gas they had pumped in to begin with. It was hard to imagine that there were not creepy crawlers down there interested in inflicting these invaders with some kind of pain. Fortunately, however, other than one of the tunnel rat's attack dogs that was the only wildlife they reported. Once you got underground it wasn't too bad, said one of their rats. "You heard all that rubbish about spiders, rats and snakes and such crap but you seldom struck anything like that."

The tunnels were kept quite clean because the Viet Cong were using them as their living quarters as well. This was not always the case because some tunnels were just the opposite and their stench was said to be overwhelming. What no one realized was how extensive this tunnel system was.

The Australian engineers took care to make detailed descriptions of the tunnel system they were exploring. Right from the first it was apparent that it was a hugely inhospitable place for Australians and Americans but it was perfectly practical for the smaller more nimble Vietnamese.

Here are some of the proportions the Aussie engineers recorded:

"The tunnel was approximately 2 feet 6 inches wide for the average tunnel. Maybe 3 feet in depth—much bigger than the main tunnel which was about 2 feet wide and about 2 feet 6 inches high in most places," said one of the engineers.

"It got smaller on turns and it was really tight when it went down another flight. The hole itself was only about 2 feet six inches in diameter and that does not give much room to change levels. It also changed directions.

"The vertical shafts went down about three feet and changed directions. In some shafts they were smaller than 2 feet 6 inches in diameter. About the same size as the trapdoors on the surface, which were about 16 inches by 13 or 14 inches."

One of their rats explained that they always went down vertical shafts feet first. There was always a place to turn off into a horizontal passageway and go head first. Right from the beginning the rats realized that these were not hurried or temporarily constructed passageways. Everything about them was done for a reason. Much thought had gone into them.

They had taken their time digging this incredibly labyrinth. One of the engineers said that the sides were not rough but good surfaces. They had taken the time to make them just right. Some parts of the tunnels had been made for special purposes because they found places where it sloped up and down and one was about 4 feet high, otherwise the average height was about 2 feet 6 inches to 3 feet.

All of the tunnels had a number of passing bays, enlargements where two crawling people could pass one another when going in opposite directions. Main tunnels had quite a few branch tunnels for side rooms where you could also be used for passing. All of the tunnels made of this hard clay with iron and aluminum content that air-dried strong as concrete. One engineer said he tried to get a bayonet into the walls and the floor but it would not go in more than an inch or two. He said it was hard as cement.

When crawling along exploring it, the roughness easily took the skin off. Especially from knees and elbows. The floors were tamped down extremely hard. They all seemed to have been heavily used.

Some parts of a tunnel, a rat could crawl through and come out covered with mud since the tunnels were often damp in different places. The booby traps were of continued concern. So the engineers were extremely careful in the tunnels. But their feeling was that they were scarce because the Viet Cong really did not expect that the allied troops would be able to follow them underground since the foreigners were so much larger than the Vietnamese. The engineers also reported that the tunnels had pegs in the tunnel walls, which they suspected might be places to string a communication link, or electrical wires.

In some cases, halfway up a wall, a root would grow down the wall across the floor and back into the earth on the other side. You can be sure such roots were carefully looked at to make sure they were roots and not trip wires.

It seemed that the only places the engineers found such traps were around the trapdoors. In one case they found a wire connected to the trapdoor with a little peg under it. The wire went through the dirt but it didn't have anything to do with the trapdoor. "Even so," said one of the Aussies, "you didn't want to open that trapdoor from below just in case."

So they followed the wire from the trapdoor and found it connected to two grenades, but the pins were not loosened as they would be for a live trap. They lifted the trapdoor and nothing happened. But that taught them to beware of all trapdoors.

When they found them in the tunnels the first thing they would do was to use their flashlights (which the Aussies and Brits call *torches*) and look carefully along their edges for wires. These trapdoors all fitted tightly and it was hard to tell if they had a wire. The next thing they did was to lift a corner of the trapdoor slightly and slip their hand in the gap feeling for wires. If they felt none, then the trapdoor was opened.

By the time these Aussie tunnel rats got themselves properly organized, there were four teams of six engineers each attached to an infantry company that had been underground in shifts from about dawn until dusk throughout the Crimp Operation. They learned new techniques and procedures every time they went down.

When this group received their orders to leave Cu Chi they had learned more about themselves and these tunnels in a week than some soldiers learned during their entire tour of duty. Considering all the tunnel exploration that went on within the engineering company's tactical area, there were also searches in the central tunnel system area that seemed to go off in all directions at once, none of these soldier had any idea how large the system was. They just knew it was BIG. This outfit had investigated it for 700 meters in one direction and 500 meters in another direction. None of them had the vaguest idea of how many more tunnels were yet to be found, but just during the week they were there on the Co Chi site they had taken out truckloads of equipment that included guns and ammunition; plus more than a half ton of documents of interest to the intelligence people. All this, but they failed to go beyond a certain trapdoor.

The day before Operation Crimp was to end and they were to be taken out of the area, two of their rats named Les and Barry had explored further down the main tunnel than anyone had ever gone before. What they found was a large trapdoor at the end of it. Carefully they checked it for booby traps. Finding none they pulled it open. It led down to a third level tunnel system which surprised them.

But at this point they were alarmed when they heard ticking suggesting they may have triggered a time bomb. The two rats thought it better for them to retreat while they still could. They called in their find to headquarters where their superior officer told them to leave it.

Since it was already late in the afternoon and the Aussie rats were underground and well out from under the battalion perimeter, battalion headquarters told them to go ahead and blow the tunnels as far as they had been explored. The idea was to prevent any Viet Cong sneaking through those tunnels and popping up inside their perimeter to attack them at night.

The next day the Americans wrapped up their operations and pulled out.

The Aussie tunnel rats went back down the tunnels to plant bags of tear gas crystals and explosives. Their intention was to destroy what they could of the tunnels and leave the rest for some future time.

They did not find out what was below that last trapdoor

until after the war many years later. The Americans assumed that the Aussies had already found the Viet Cong headquarters and destroyed it. But they had not. What they destroyed was but a small part of a tunnel system that incredibly stretched out for 300 kilometers!

The trapdoor that Les and Barry found was the gateway to that third level of tunnels which was the military headquarters of the Viet Cong's southern command. And at the far end of that they would have been close to finding the heart of the Viet Cong's entire operation, everything underground. The Viet Cong had not the slightest suspicion that the Allies would ever be able to follow them into those tunnels. That's why all the equipment and documents were concealed there.

Interestingly the Viet Cong had been ordered by their superior not to attack any enemy soldiers that entered the tunnel system for fear that they might attract too much attention to it and learn how incredibly vital it was to their military efforts. Had Barry and Les pursued their way into that third level of tunnels they most certainly would have been killed. Had that happened, the secret of why the Viet Cong didn't want us there would probably become known.

The Viet Cong had pulled back as far as they could in the tunnels. Had they been discovered there, it would have led to a dreadful loss of lives for both sides. Historians have already speculated that their discovery might have changed the outcome of the war, which the Allies would have won.

They think that if the Allies had not shut down their exploration of these tunnels and thereby missed their chance of uncovering the core of the entire enemy operation, it might have changed the course of the war.

The Viet Cong planned the Tet Offensive of 1968 while occupying those tunnels. The assault upon Saigon was made by troops hidden in them. That network of tunnels had eventually expanded from 300 kilometers to 600 kilometers. That's how important they were to the North Vietnamese

Army.

Had their secret underground headquarters been discovered by the Tunnel Rats the enemy would have come under extremely heavy aerial bombardments. The Allies could have smashed the military might of the enemy's war machine and dealt a crushing blow to the enemy's morale as well.

According to North Vietnamese military leaders interviewed after the war, they had 5,000 troops in those tunnels at various times. It was learned that some of them had been there for up to six months and had not seen the light of day throughout that time. For many of those tunnel dwellers who survived the war they found they no longer could tolerate the intense light of day.

If we had understood how extensive this underground network was and how important it was to the other side, the war might have ended much sooner. Such was the value of this very complex network of secret tunnels and storage areas underground.

10

THE TUNNEL

(Reprinted from the author's e-book ROLLING THUNDER)

One of the things that puzzled our early troops fighting in Vietnam was how the North Vietnamese Army had a way of suddenly opening up out of nowhere in the jungle, firing hot and heavy from cover, slamming us with a red-hot firefight in which no one really got a clear shot at any of the enemy, then like ghosts they all disappeared just as quickly behind the smoke and fog of battle, leaving behind nothing but the dead, the wounded, and a lot of wild-eyed guys wondering what the hell just hit them.

This kind of thing happened so often that it almost jinxed our guys. Nobody could figure how they did it. The enemy was a bunch of little guys in funny hats that blended right in with all that greenery and they seemed to be able to come and go wherever they wanted. In front of, behind, or from our flanks, all blasting away with their AK-47s and mowing down our good guys left and right. Then they all disappeared. Crazier than that they all went to war dressed in black silk pajamas! Now how weird is *that*?

Nobody could figure it out. The enemy could pop up anywhere amidst all that green vegetation, ambush our troops with a withering deadly fire, then drop out of sight again. Just like that. Too spooky to think about. And it sure was racking up a lot of casualties for the home team.

Then, after awhile, the good guys began to find small covered camouflaged places on the jungle floor that when their covers were removed they led into tunnels. These turned off into a whole fan of tunnels that proved to be more complex than those ant farms kids used to buy. Between two walls of glass you saw ants burrowing all over the place. That's what there seemed to be beneath those miles of tangled vines and wild jungle – tunnels under their feet that went everywhere. And now we knew how those small fleet-footed fellows in their funny hats and slinky silk pajamas came and went when we least suspected it. While the troops moved cautiously through their jungle topside trying to avoid all the hidden traps they laid for us, they were sneaking along their underground passageways just waiting to spring up out of one of their wormholes and shoot us. What a helluva way to fight a war!

It was the end of August when a tunnel rat asked Wilder if he would be interested in looking into a tunnel complex they had recently found to see what it contained. Wilder was not too interested in exploring any unexplored tunnels that the troops had found in Arizona Territory. Yet he was curious about those places and what they might contain. Most of the really complex tunnel systems had been built laboriously as far back as the 1940s. Villagers dug them out of the clay at an incredibly slow rate of speed … about five or six feet a day. Considering that some of these labyrinths were said to go on for miles underground their construction was no small thing. They were said to contain entire hospitals where the wounded were taken care of just meters under the troops' boots.

Entire regiments could be down there and move from sector to sector without our men knowing anything about it. That was of course how they appeared and disappeared so quickly to our combat troops. It gave the enemy quite an advantage. We might rule the skies with our Air Force but the Vietnamese ruled the underground complexes. The tunnels hid their weapons, their large food supplies, their hospitals and their troops during the daylight hours when they were especially subject to aerial attacks, as well as firefights with our roving patrols. One reason why those who were in those combat areas felt that the nights belonged to Charlie was because that's when they appeared above ground and caused trouble. The VC knew that at the end of the day most GIs returned to their bases, put down their weapons and had chow. If they weren't on duty they retired to their bunkers and relaxed for the night. So that's why the night belonged to Charlie. Supplies moved down the Ho Chi Minh Trail like soldier ants carrying supplies and following one another. Quietly and efficiently. They did it all in the dark. By smearing stuff they made from fireflies on the back of the pack of the man ahead of them they followed the dim bluish glow. Clever.

Our guys who thrived on checking out the underground tunnels were called Tunnel Rats. Since the tunnel openings were built just to accommodate the small stature of the Vietnamese people, most Americans were too big to even get into the things. So it often fell to the smaller ones among them to go it alone. They deserved medals for that duty because the places were often booby-trapped and rigged with all manner of bizarre critters that liked nothing better than to bite an interloper in the pitch black hot and humid black hole of their quirky tunnels. One story that made its rounds described a rat making his way cautiously into one of the recently discovered rat holes with flashlight in one hand and .45 in the other. If he was an old hand at it he probably was already half deaf from firing the .45 in such a confined space and having his ears ring for the next few days. Reason why if they were specialists in poking around these rat holes they wrote home for a small caliber handgun before they lost their hearing entirely.

Since any newly found tunnel by our troops was usually treated to a fragmentation grenade or two to minimize the chance that one or more VC might be hidden there, the openings were often blasted larger. The first thing tunnel rats did was to carefully check the floor and walls for booby traps.

One story making its rounds was about the rat who found

two very basic grenade traps with their pins pulled almost all of the way out and just needed someone to put his hand or knee on the concealed wire that would complete the job. The guy said, after that he checked the tunnel ahead of him with his flashlight and it looked clear, except that there were a number of roots hanging down from the ceiling.

As he crawled closer he half-consciously thought he saw some of the roots moving. When he shined his light on them he found that each one was a deadly viper called a three-step snake. Looking more like a green shoelace they got their name from the belief that first you stepped on them; with the second step they bit you and with your third step you fell down dead. This guy knew how to handle these deadly vipers so he was happy to see them. His hobby was to collect the snakes so he could drop them down the bamboo ventilators of other tunnels as a surprise for the tunnel inhabitants. These he picked off the roots they had been tied to and dropped them into a leather ball bag of a water buffalo he always carried with him for his slithery pets.

When one of the tunnel rats asked Wilder if he would like to see one of the tunnels they had just found, the sniper's curiosity got the best of him.

"Sure, I'll go with you," said Wilder, "if I can fit into the thing."

"No worry," said the rat. "We widened the opening with grenades, but you're skinny enough."

Wilder borrowed a .45 and followed the rat into what looked like a regular bunker. He was on his hands and knees and had no problem getting into the tunnel. The only thing he didn't like was its smell. The fumes from the grenades were pretty strong. The two crawled slowly as the rat ahead of Wilder checked the sides and the floor with his bayonet searching for any possible booby trap. Wilder kept his light off and left some wiggle room between himself and the rat.

As they moved deeper into the tunnel both of them were sweating freely from the heavy humidity, yet there was a certain pleasant coolness to it that they appreciated.

As they moved deeper into the tunnel the feeling of claustrophobia was slowly closing in on Wilder. He didn't like being in such tight places. But his buddy was so used to it that he didn't mind it at all. In fact, he earlier told Wilder that tunnel crawling through tight passageways made him feel safe and secure.

It was just the opposite for Wilder. Here they were crawling underground in a dark, smelly place where anything could happen. They could be buried alive in an instant death trap. It didn't help either that Wilder's only view of that trap was the rear end of the grunt leading him deeper into it. Still, the sniper's heart thumped faster from the excitement of exploring the unknown. What would they find? What was hidden there?

They would crawl for a distance then stop, turn off their flashlights and listen. They heard nothing but silence. But when they moved they heard soft scurrying noises ahead of them. Wilder shivered, guessing what that meant. Tunnel rats! The real kind.

Eventually the tunnel angled downhill, deeper underground. It occurred to Wilder that there might be a reason why it was doing this. The best reason he could thing of was that the tunnel-builders wanted to put more earth between them and any potential danger from artillery or overhead bombing.

Eventually, the tunnel opened up to the point where they could stand up as they entered a large cavern-like chamber filled with wicker baskets and containers of all kinds of stuff. There were other tunnels leading out of this main room, so there were probably other ways to reach the room they had found. It looked like they were in the main hub of a huge underground storage area full of supplies.

Wilder guessed that it might be many years old because from the looks of things they had not been disturbed since the day were hidden there. As the two moved their light beams around this chamber Wilder had the strange feeling they were in Egypt and they were exploring some long-forgotten tomb and were about to find a treasure trove.

The two moved around looking more closely at what was there, probing into the containers with the beams of their lights. They found dozens of large wicker baskets of rice. Food supplies for their troops. The closer they looked the more amazed they were at what they found. There were all kinds of paper documents and maps in one area stored in containers and sometimes there were documents hidden down under the rice. The two men stuffed their pockets with documents. They found lots of AK-47 rifles and boxes of ammunition. Besides that were baskets full of paper money along with coins and crates of medical supplies. But what really caught Wilder's attention were the many large boxes containing long bolts of black silk for making the pajama-like VC clothes that they wore There had to be hundreds of rolls of this black Chinese silk that would have been worth a fortune back in the world.

The two loaded up on documents, paper money and coins then they crawled back to the entrance of the tunnel again. They moved faster this time no longer concerned with booby traps because there were none. That might have meant that the tunnel was being used many times by the VC to replenish their stores.

Once the two men emerged from the tunnel, everyone listened excitedly to what they had found. Then the grunts crawled in to bring out the weapons and the ammo. After that, the demolition boys moved in with their rigged C4 setups. Once the explosives were in place and everyone was above ground, they blew the whole thing up.

Wilder thought about all the rice and medical supplies along with hundreds of bolts of valuable Chinese black silk that had just gone up in smoke. All gone.

He did not feel good about that part of it.

11

Last Words

Trying to talk the enemy out of a tunnel, telling them that they would not be harmed was always a tricky situation. Some might be willing to come out; others night be determined to stay inside and to take their chances.

In one case several enemy were known to be hiding in a tunnel Marines had uncovered. Their Vietnamese Kit Carson interpreter talked to the tunnel inhabitants. He told them that if they surrendered they would not be hurt but would be held with other prisoners. Eventually, five of them crawled out blinking in the sunlight. They were North Vietnamese Army soldiers. Their AK-47s were taken away from them. The interpreter asked if there were any more of them in the tunnel. They said no, they were the only ones.

So the Marines tossed in a couple hand grenades just in case. When the dust settled and the fumes were no longer a problem a tunnel rat was called in to check it out.

Leaving his pack, long rifle and dog tags with their someone topside, the small soldier grasped his .45 in his right hand, his light in his left and he began squirming through to the inside of the tunnel. Hardly ten feet from the entrance, those outside heard him curse, then the rat reappeared at the tunnel opening saying there was a wounded man in the passageway.

The Marines figured the easiest way to get him out was to dig down from outside. They moved a little beyond where they thought his body was and dug. Shortly the ceiling gave way and fell down, exposing the tunnel. At the same instant a grenade was tossed up into the rescuers who immediately dived for cover. The grenade fell back into the tunnel and detonated on the guy who threw it.

After things settled down the relieved Marines finally hauled the unconscious soldier out of his hole. He was seriously wounded.

Surprisingly, he came too and began verbally scolding the Marines. They just sat there while their prisoner talked and their Kit Carson scout translated what he said. The man spoke softly because he was weakening. He told them that they were fighting for the wrong side. He said that the Viet Cong was fighting to help the poor people and that the Americans should not be in Vietnam, that they should leave them alone to settle their own political problems.

The Marines waited. They just sat listening to him in silence. The North Vietnamese soldier talked for forty-five minutes before he died from his injuries. None of the Marines believed it then, but many years later, those who cared, learned that he had spoken the truth.

12

Buried Alive

Percival Christopher Wren, the author of such adventure classics as *Beau Geste,* and other great adventure stories about the French Foreign Legion, described how the nomadic Toareg Arabs of the Sahara Desert treated any Legionnaire they captured. First they carefully sliced off his eyelids with a sharp knife. Then they buried him in an ant hill and poured honey over his head. The following Tunnel Rat's tale reminded me of that particularly bad ending.

Based on a Grandson's description of his Grandpa's experiences as a Tunnel Rat during the Vietnam War, I have left out some of the more graphic events he described to keep you from up chucking.

Anyone who has ever been entirely buried and immobilized by snow, quicksand or landslide knows what total helplessness is. He also knows the taste of real fear for circumstances that almost always end badly. But neither snow, nor quicksand have the added torment to the victim of being slowly nibbled to death by some of our most fearsome creepy-crawlers.

Here's the way this tunnel tale started: Our hero for this story was a brand new tunnel rat I'll call Dan, newly drafted and just out of boot, a short, skinny wide-eyed kid new to Nam. He hardly got off the plane when an officer spotted him and made some remark about his size. He asked Dan if he wanted to make an extra 50 bucks by volunteering for a job he alone could do. Dan said sure, and before he knew it he was the company's first new tunnel rat. It just involved squirming down into a black hole in the ground and shooting anyone he found there. He hadn't found anyone there yet but he thought he could handle it.

That's the way it happened in his first three tunnels, all of them short and empty. More like basements under huts.

Now, with two grunts along in case he needed help, he was ready to clear his next tunnel. Dan left his pack, rifle and tags with his buddies and with a small caliber handgun and flashlight he wriggled into the hole. Once in the horizontal tunnel a few feet from the entrance he clipped the GI-issue angled head Fulton flashlight to his belt and waited while his eyes adjusted to the dark. Then he crawled maybe 20 feet when he suddenly heard two shots. He didn't know it then but a VC sniper, shooting through a slot in another tunnel, killed both of his backup buddies outside!

Underground, after Dan heard the shots and his buddies' cries, he broke out in a cold sweat and started breathing hard. Half-expecting the enemy to come in after him, he waited and worried in the darkness. After five minutes when none came, Dan decided to crawl deeper into the tunnel. Maybe outside, the enemy would go somewhere else.

It was the monsoon season and afternoon downpours were common. All of the local streams were running fast and higher than usual. None of the other tunnels Dan had been in seemed anything more than short, fairly shallow hiding places usually associated with a grass hut, a place where a VC could hide until it was safe to come out to join others on a night raid against the Americans. It began raining hard outside and he felt water running down the tunnel floor.

This tunnel was different than the others. It had some sharp bends to it. Dan continued crawling through the darkness keeping his flashlight on his belt as he carefully felt the sides and floor ahead of him for any trip wires alerting him to a booby trap. He became a bit alarmed when he felt the rainwater growing deeper.

This turned out to be a much longer tunnel than Dan had

ever explored before. In the distance he heard what sounded like a lot of running water. From the hollow roar it made, he thought there might be a large room ahead with a stream flowing through it. But none appeared. The sound of rushing water grew louder but Dan had no idea what was causing it.

Suddenly the tunnel made an abrupt turn. He glimpsed light ahead where the tunnel had caved in. To his horror he saw rushing water pouring into the end of the tunnel that angled downward away from him. He had to get out of where he was because if the water backed up into his part of the tunnel he would drown. If he got caught in that torrent where the cave-in was he could be pushed deeper into the flooded tunnel where he would never be able to swim out. He needed to escape *now!* But how?

He figured he was only about two and a half feet underground. That's all he would have to dig straight up to be out of danger. He felt overhead. The clay was sticky and dripping.

Shoving his handgun into his belt he went at it frantically, clawing at the ceiling of what he now thought of as his tomb. He began making headway but it was slow and he realized the swift torrents were gradually eating their way back toward him.

That made him speed up in a hurry. He clawed his way upward into the gradually giving ground. It was further than he thought. His fingernails broke and his fingertips were raw but he felt no pain. His adrenaline had kicked in. When he felt the ground shake he knew some force greater than him was beginning to move those tunnel walls!

With one violent grinding roar, half of the tunnel between him and the rushing water caved in. His whole body felt the collapse around him, while his hands frantically grabbed at the heavy earth falling down on him as he was trying to struggle up through it, pushing and kicking hard with his legs.

Suddenly he saw light overhead as the earth cracked open

above him. He gasped for air. *He was going to make it!* He saw the small opening and redoubled his efforts to get to it, his one tiny window of life!

As he did a slow motion crawl through the shifting reddish heavy clay around him, he managed to get one arm and his head into the opening just below that window. Then everything around his body clamped down on him like a giant vise. His body was in a twisted sprawl position where he couldn't move anything but his head, shoulder and part of his left arm. His left shoulder was out but his left arm was buried, reaching for that opening above him. His hand was numb and his forearm seemed paralyzed. His other buried arm was under him locked against his right side.

More noises of cave-ins followed but this time the sounds were further ahead of him as the rushing muddy waters collapsed the more distant parts of the tunnel. He thanked God for it being there and not where he was. But he was stuck so tight he could move just his upper left arm from his elbow to his shoulder. He was buried alive in the middle of a wilderness where nobody knew what had happened to him.

In a panic his mind raced. It immediately locked onto his older brother Bud and what had happened to him. To celebrate their high-school graduation he and his buddy Rick chartered a big game hunting guide to fly them into an extremely remote area of Quebec to hunt moose. They had done this and hunted that area before. It was a dismal wilderness country filled with bogs, swamps, and lots of game. They were the only ones there. The guide would fly back a week later to pick them up.

As the plane circled where they planned to camp, Bud spotted a big moose near their site and he wanted to go after him. So while Rick set up camp, Bud went off to see if he could get a shot at the moose.

Rick never saw him again. He never came back. He never fired his rifle or called for help. Rick searched and searched. All he knew was that the wilderness had somehow just swallowed him up. If Bud had gotten lost, he would have fired his rifle so Rick could find him. If Bud had dropped dead from a heart attack, Rick would have found his body because he didn't have time to go far from their camp site.

Finally, when Rick couldn't come up with any answer to his friend's disappearance, he radioed for help and other searchers joined him.

When word reached his home town, Dan and a bunch of Bud's high-school buddies flew up to Quebec and joined the search, hoping to find some trace of him before winter's heavy snows covered everything.

But they found nothing. The search continued the following spring but nothing was ever found. Their only guess was that Bud may have stepped into one of the bottomless bogs and was unable to get out before anyone came looking for him. Now, his brother Dan felt just as helpless.

Dan wanted to call out, but he was afraid the enemy would hear and would finish him off quickly. He kept moving what he could but that wasn't much. Then suddenly he realized that things were moving around his head. As soon as he felt them climbing up on his face he knew what they were. The water had flooded a colony of black ants and now they were running around frantically trying to investigate this strange intruder in their world.

Chills went through him as he felt them crawling through his hair and onto his face. Thankfully they weren't the big red ones that everyone feared in Nam. These were not biting ants but they could sure tickle you to death. Those that crawled up his nose he snorted out. Those on his lips he quickly licked off and swallowed. It might be a long time before he got anything to eat and he didn't mind swallowing any of these if only they would just leave him alone.

Before long the tiny black nuisances lost interest and left him. Dan gave a sigh of relief and began trying to move his buried body even if just a little bit. When he realized he had to take a leak he went ahead and did it. Maybe in a small way it would wash away some of the surrounding dirt. Despite the relief he felt he began to worry that the pungent odor of urine might attract other creepy-crawlers to the feast.

Hours passed and despite his efforts he knew he was going to be there for a long time unless some kind of miracle happened. Fat chance of that since nobody knew where he was or what happened. Worst, he was helpless to do anything about it. He learned that when small flies began zeroing in on his warm, moist exposed armpit and eyes.

Blinking kept them out of his eyes but not his exposed armpit. They had about an inch opening at his shirtsleeve. A few got in and then about 30 of the hungry buggers followed. Moving his shoulder didn't seem to bother them. Whether it was the warm moisture or what, he could only guess, but they repeatedly bit him and it was extremely painful. It reminded him of being bitten by a horsefly when he was a kid. Just multiply that thirty times!

As the sun began to set most of the flies left but he still felt a few of them remaining there crawling around in the hair of his armpit. He wanted to scream but he smothered it.

As night came on so too did swarms of bloodthirsty mosquitoes. There was nothing he could do to prevent it. There were black clouds of them funneling down into his air pocket. He heard the loud hum hundreds of them made as they fought to find an open place to feed on him. They settled on every inch of exposed skin, sank their drills into him and drank their fill of his warm blood. He felt each and every one of their bites and he bit his lips in agony until he tasted blood. Wave after wave of them came in and attacked him for a sip of his blood while he huffed and puffed and squirmed in agony, totally frustrated that he couldn't wipe them off and flay his arms about to drive them away. But he couldn't. He was completely at their mercy; defenseless, until they bled him dry. Maybe at least then he would black out and no longer feel their pain. Oh how he wanted that blissful peace of death. But it didn't come. He couldn't take much more of things eating him alive. He knew he would go screaming insane with the torment.

By dawn most of them, their bodies bloated with his blood, managed to take off for the shade as the sun soon came up. During that brief moment of peace, he mercifully fell asleep, his dreams filled with the horrors of his experience going over and over in his subconscious like a repeating nightmare. In his dreams he heard screaming, but he didn't know who it was.

As daylight came on, so too did a new batch of hungry insects. He woke up with a start. So far he had managed to avoid the attention of Vietnam's giant centipede that was as long as a man's forearm and big around as a beer bottle. The pain of its bite was said to be terrible. One of Dan's buddies put one of them in a guy's bunk as a joke and it bit the guy several times before the others managed to kill it. Dan had always hated the small ones he saw in his basement that were only a couple inches long. These were giants and like the small ones, they all had a million pointed tan-colored legs running down both sides of their beer-bottle-brown segmented bodies. Just the thought of something like that around you gave everyone the creeps. Now Dan was lying there helpless in that monster's backyard. He prayed it never found him.

This thought got him busy trying to free himself from the earth's grip. By trying to work his fingers, feeling gradually came back into his buried left hand and forearm. Once he got his fingers moving they soon dug their way out. Working hard he managed to get his entire left arm uncovered. By reaching up and stretching he could just get his left hand out the opening overhead. The thought immediately came to him that maybe by grabbing the edge of the hole and pulling he could pull himself out of this mess.

But his fumbling around the edge of the opening brought

down an avalanche of loose dirt and debris on his face. Frightened that he might get dirt in his eyes and not be able to see, he stopped.

The funnel-shaped opening above him provided him with air but he saw at once that his head and left shoulder were at the bottom of that funnel. If it rained it wouldn't take much to drown him. And if that narrow shaft within his reach washed in or caved in, he was a goner. He wouldn't be buried alive anymore. He'd just be buried ….

Abruptly, he saw the other disadvantage of this narrow window of light when more dirt fell on him long after he had already pulled back his arm.

Squinting and looking up Dan saw the very thing he had just been dreading. First he saw its ugly head with its long probing forelegs. It paused as though smelling or seeing him.

Dan's heart lurched when he saw the ugly head of the giant centipede pausing and looking down at him. Then, it slithered the full length of its two-foot-long scaly, many-legged body into his hole and in a shower of dirt and leaves, it fell toward him.

Instinctively Dan's left arm shot out and grabbed it in midair just before the thing landed on his face. It instantly doubled over in his grasp and bit him on the back of his hand. Dan screamed. The pain felt as though someone had just shot him in the hand. He responded by squeezing for all his might on that squirming thing with all its legs grabbing at his arm and fingers as he crushed it in his grip.

As the giant centipede's body burst in his hand it showered his face with the foulest liquid you can imagine. Still squirming with all of its million legs going a mile a minute both parts of its mangled remains fell onto his face.

Dan vomited what little he had in his stomach all over the centipede and whatever parts of himself that were exposed at the bottom of that hellhole.

When that horror finally subsided, Dan was still gagging with dry heaves at what had just happened. As he began thinking rationally again, he wondered how much worse he had just made it for himself. Now, his vomit and the smell of the centipede's remains instantly attracted a swarm of more uninvited vermin to the feast – the flies covered the guts. Right behind them came a huge big red ant. Dan's gut-smeared hand grabbed that intruder too and squashed the life out of it.

Well, almost. The hairy squashed body landed near his tightly closed mouth and in its death throes it bit Dan's lip. Again Dan heard someone wildly screaming and was in such torment from the pain that he never realized they were his screams.

To make matters worse if that were possible Dan now felt there was considerable activity underground around his crotch area where a million tiny stinging, burning bites were taking place all over his genitals. This time he knew who was screaming and trying desperately to move his lower region. Desperately he tried to avoid the furious attack from a disturbed bed of fire ants. But it was useless. The tiny red demons whose bites felt like miniature red-hot pokers continued to sting him all over his gonads and rectum. It was at that insanely awful moment of torment that Dan mercifully passed out.

How long he was unconscious he never learned. He remembered waking up in the middle of the night feeling as though his crotch was on fire with pain as hoards of mosquitoes covered all of his exposed parts and began feeding on him. But what woke him was not the terrible agony that he felt all over his buried body; it was the shock of realizing it was raining.

Oh how he welcomed it now, licking the precious drops off his swollen, cracked lips hoping that it would pour down heavy enough to fill his hole until he drowned in all that welcome water. That's when he knew how badly he wanted to die.

He got his wish. It poured hard. Mercifully he passed out

and let nature do its job. In the total darkness that came over him he saw a great white bright light glaring at him in the distance and he figured at last he was now going to find out what came after death. He was no longer in pain. Blissfully he felt at peace. He felt wonderful. But he did wonder why heaven was thundering when the rain had stopped.

As the clouds slowly cleared from his confused brain he realized it wasn't heaven at all. The bright light was from his hole overhead. He was still in Nam. He heard gunfire. It got closer. He didn't care who was making it, he had to attract their attention. It was his last chance to get out of this living hell.

Reaching for the window of light overhead he got his hand out. He waved it frantically as his cracking voice called for help over and over ....

Suddenly he heard someone exclaim, *"Oh my God!"*

Staring up at that window of white light Dan saw the face of the angel that had come to save him. Looking shocked back at him was the unshaven face of his Top they all called Batman.

"Danny Boy, what the hell are you doing down there?" yelled his first sergeant.

Those were the sweetest words Dan would ever hear.

His men swiftly dug him out and medevaced him to a hospital where doctors treated wounds all over his body. The toughest ones were in his armpit where botflies had laid their eggs expecting him to be the perfect host for another generation of those flying devils.

In time his wounds healed and Dan returned to his old outfit to finish out his service as a highly respected Tunnel Rat.

When Dan was discharged and finally went back to the world, all he had to show for his service as a Tunnel Rat in Vietnam were tiny scars all over his body. He never told anyone what happened to him for many years. But when his young Grandson kept asking, he finally broke his silence and unburdened himself to his family.

They were appalled. His Grandson was the only one who liked hearing the story over and over again. He bragged to all of his friends about his incredibly heroic Grandpa who had fought valiantly as a tough Tunnel Rat during the war. Only after Dan told his loved ones what happened to him in Vietnam did his nightmares finally begin to leave him.

13

Batman and Flowers

By mid 1968 we largely understood how important the tunnel system was to our enemy. If there was one important thing we learned from Operation Cedar Falls, the Army's effort to mop up some of these underground redoubts, it was the decision to not allow untrained men to explore tunnels. Too many deaths had already occurred from doing that. At the time, our only organized tunnel rat team was part of the First Infantry Division – the Big Red One. This bunch of tunnel rats was formerly created in June 1967 when it was initially an offshoot of the Intelligence and Reconnaissance Section of the First Engineer Battalion. These guys got busy with a vengeance.

The team was commanded by a lieutenant known as Rat 6, that number a division's code for the battalion's commander. Nicknamed the Diehard 6, this Tunnel Rat patrol also was known as The Diehard Tunnel Rats.

The team had two sergeants. One was Sergeant Robert Batten who had been assigned to them at the beginning. Batten volunteered for two extra tours of duty because he liked doing what he did so well, remaining in Vietnam for three years. Of course with a name like that the sergeant quickly became known as "Batman."

In his mid-twenties with red hair and hailing from New Jersey, Sergeant Batten was the most experienced, most respected, and most feared of all the tunnel rats we had. He was the one who earned the elite reputation these Diehard Tunnel Rats came to enjoy. Under him that team was to account for over one hundred enemy dead. Batman was so hated by the enemy that the Viet Cong listed him as one of ten most wanted after our generals. In fact he was the only non-commissioned officer on that list. Most Viet Cong knew who Batman was, and feared him for good reason – they couldn't take him out. They might with luck wound him, but in the end he and his men always won. Batman was one of those people you sometimes met during your time in combat who always came out smelling like roses. Soldiers like that always led charmed lives, we thought. But the truth was that they were one hell of a good soldier who oftentimes made their own luck.

All of the men on Batman's team were volunteers who would serve only a year. The average man among them served four months. There were about seven or eight men in a Tunnel Rat squad and they each received an additional fifty dollars a month hazardous duty pay.

Each of the teams – and there were two of them – had their own medics, radio operators and Kit Carson translators – two per team. These native translators were Vietnamese teenagers who learned their expertise after having been with the Viet Cong in their early years. They were given a limited amount of trust but were never allowed to be on point (Lead man on any mission.)

Each team of rats was on standby and could be helicoptered into any area where tunnels were found that needed to be cleaned out. They could be rappelled (roped down) in jungle areas where no landing zones were available. They spent their nights back at their base camp.

These trained tunnel rats seldom encountered the enemy but when they did they took them out. Since many tunnels were used for hiding supplies, the rats recovered an enormous amount of rice, ammunition, explosives, stored weapons and important intelligence documents from them. Once the tunnels were cleaned out they were destroyed.

In 1969, a college dropout from Indiana who had been

drafted and who had gone through the Officer Candidate School (OCS) was invited to volunteer as a Rat 6 with Batman's team of tunnel rats. Lieutenant Jack Flowers eagerly took the job. He was a rough, tough, short fellow with spiky hair who was now expected to command an elite group of specialists who already had a highly respected veteran leader.

Not a comfortable mix. Batman was mean, aggressive and a decorated war hero who knew what it took to stay alive in this deadly tunnel game. Now, here was this rookie officer who out-ranked Batman and who knew nothing about this kind of warfare. Not intending to lead from behind a desk, this fellow wanted to be a hands-on officer who would lead his team into the tunnels as their Point Man.

Well aware of the possible conflict, Lieutenant Flowers spelled it out to his First Sergeant as soon as he took command of the group. He said, "I'll give you thirty days to teach me what I need to know about this business, and then I intend being Point Man for this outfit."

You can imagine how that went over with Batman, the tough little hard-headed long-recognized veteran leader of this elite rat pack. These guys were his creation; **his** family.

Understandably Flowers' attitude rubbed Batman the wrong way. But somehow they settled their differences and found they made a remarkable team together. That became evident in this single most memorable underground adventure:

On the 26th of March 1969 the tunnel rats were called into action. North Vietnamese Army soldiers were seen entering a tunnel complex after a fierce firefight near the Saigon River. A tank commander followed them into the tunnel but was immediately killed by a booby trap. When Flowers and the team arrived on the spot, Batman with one of the team members entered the tunnel.

Moments later Flowers and the others heard shots and grenade explosions deep underground. After a few minutes Batman appeared at the entrance where he had dragged his companion who was bleeding from shrapnel wounds to his arms and legs. The two were hauled out of the tunnel and the medics went to work.

Batman told Flowers that after a brief skirmish inside, the enemy had escaped through a trapdoor in the ceiling of the tunnel and was sitting on it. Batman said, "They've got us shut out."

Flowers looked at his sergeant, "What do you suggest?"

"We need to go back in and somehow breech that trapdoor," said Batman.

"Then I'm coming along," said Flowers. "It was one of my men they wounded."

"Okay," said Batman. "Gear up and follow me."

When the two got to the trapdoor in the ceiling, smoke and acrid fumes from the grenade still hung heavy in the air, making their eyes smart.

Batman braced his back against the trapdoor. Pushing with his legs he shoved the door upward. As soon as he could he thrust his handgun through the opening and fired.

Then he followed with his light.

"Give me your pistol!"

Flowers shoved it into his hand. He swiftly re-loaded Batman's weapon.

Apparently the North Vietnamese Army soldier who had been sitting on the door had left. The two tunnel rats were determined to stay on his tail and to get this guy if they could. But this decision amped up the danger level considerably.

Batman knew this from experience. Nothing was more dangerous that a fleeing enemy who now knew he was being followed. He knew every inch of that tunnel. He knew how and where he could arm booby traps. He knew where his hides were; where he could lie in wait to attack them. He knew places where the trapdoors themselves could lock behind the followers so they would suffocate. He knew everything that they didn't know which made their decision that much closer to being a fatal one.

At least Batman was aware of these things. They didn't worry Flowers. He was just following along. Batman would look after him. He felt sure of himself. He hadn't lived as long as he had without taking chances. So far his luck had held. Would it this time? Would it for them both? That was a stretch. A lot was against them now. But Batman knew they had to try.

Flowers followed a safe distance behind Batman as he squirmed through the winding passageway in the dark. That safe distance was out of range of the flying shrapnel that would pepper the person who triggered it first and hopefully miss the man several body lengths behind the one getting the full blast.

Batman crawled ahead and soon came upon another trapdoor. This one on the floor. Flowers saw Batman do the same thing with this trapdoor. He lifted it partway, reached through with his handgun and fired.

Suddenly, the ugly muzzle of an automatic weapon was thrust up through the opening and as quickly as it appeared it began spitting out hot lead.

Both men were showered by flying dirt. The noise was deafening. Batman immediately fell backwards toward Flowers who thought he had been hit.

He crawled to the sergeant but amazingly he was unhurt. Dirt had sprayed in his face and he was trying to get it out of his eyes.

Batman pointed toward the foot square opening in the floor. "Shoot in there," he said. Flowers fired three shots as quickly as he could pull the trigger and swiftly reloaded while Batman began talking to himself, "Those sons of bitches," he said. "Here they are trying to kill me again."

He tried to crawl pass Flowers who was blocking his way to the trapdoor. But Flowers held him back, "Uh-uh. Nope. You had your two trapdoors. Now I get mine!"

They made a rule that because of the high stress of these things each rat got two trapdoors to try to get through. After that another team member got the trapdoor duty for their two. Besides, Batman looked a little batty to Flowers from everything that had happened. Mainly they were both suffering for being too close to loud explosions. Their ears were about to ring off their heads.

When Flowers said that it was his turn out front on point, Batman moved aside as the lieutenant squeezed pass him and went through the open trapdoor.

As he crawled down to the next level, Flowers fired three more shots into the darkness just in case. Then three more as he approached a bend on his knees. Flashlight held off to his left side; gun pointed at the bend on his right; he heard Batman crawling down behind him.

No one jumped them at the bend. It was tight and they sweated their way around it listening in the dark for any sounds of movement.

After that the tunnel straightened out for the next ten yards. Then, to all appearances it stopped at a blank wall.

"What the devil? Where'd that guy go?" thought Flowers.

"Typical vanishing act," thought Batman. "He's here somewhere but where?"

The two of them studied the blank clay wall, feeling for any suspected booby traps or hidden doors. The wall felt perfectly solid and there wasn't a hidden trapdoor anywhere they could see. They checked it carefully with their flashlights.

A small amount of dirt sifted down from above. Looking up they saw the faint outline of a rectangular trapdoor.

Flowers kept his flashlight shining on that door. While he did, Batman, with his pistol ready, tried to push it up and open. Its failure to move suggested that the soldier they were chasing was probably sitting on it making it impossible for them to budge.

Batman moved up beside Flowers and was going to join Flowers in trying to lift it but the lieutenant stopped him. Batman stared at Flowers, who was now Rat 6 the Pont Man.

Flowers said, "Back off. I'll handle this myself."

Batman knew he couldn't argue with the man who was now Rat 6 in charge of the situation. So he crawled back a few yards.

Flowers wiped the sweat out of his eyes and summoned all the strength he could. He backed up against the wall and sat under the trapdoor a foot over his head. Placing the flashlight between his legs so that it shined upward on the door he slid his hand under the edge of the door and began gradually to leverage it up.

Neither of them whispered a word. Flowers inhaled, nodded to Batman that he was again going to give it a serious push.

When he did, it gave and as it moved upward he twisted it so that it sat crossways on its wood frame. At that point he paused, intending to shove it aside and start firing into that empty space above him. But before he could do that, the trapdoor that he had just pushed up and turned sideways silently turned back the way it was and dropped back into its frame.

Flowers stiffened when he saw that. He knew the guy they were chasing was right there above them.

Unexpectedly the door moved again. Something dropped into Flower's lap. He saw it in slow motion as you might in a movie, saw it falling slowly frame by slow-motion frame the object falling … falling … falling … and he knew instantly what it was. He screamed, *"Grenade!"*

It was one of their own, a captured American M-26 hand grenade with its segmented steel casting over a coil of pressed steel, the inner coil designed to separate into 700 pieces to join the chunks of segmented metal sections of its outer shell to become deadly flying chunks of jagged hot metal that would tear human flesh to shreds. And it could do this up to fifteen feet. It would detonate when the pin was pulled releasing its handle and igniting the acid fuse that did its deadly business in anywhere from five to seven seconds before the detonator set off its pound of high explosive.

Seeing that falling grenade dropping in excruciatingly slow motion into his lap was the heart-stopping nightmare Lieutenant Jack Flowers would sweat through every night for the rest of his life!

He never knew how far he crawled, scrambled or clawed before the explosion shattered the silence of the tunnel. He just remembered the terrible ringing in his ears and the feeling of warm blood running down his legs as he continued wildly crawling through the tunnels.

He was hurriedly leaving the area when Flowers reached Batman who shined his light on Flower's shredded bloody fatigues and knew they had to get out of there in a hurry. *"Keep moving!"* Batman urged.

Dazed from the explosion Flowers was babbling about losing his pistol. Batman said, "Forget it. Just keep moving!"

Another explosion shattered the tunnel behind them. The NVA (North Vietnamese Army) soldier wanted to be sure that they were dead. They were leaving a heavy blood trail. Batman kept glancing over his shoulder. Twice he fired a couple rounds behind them to warn off any pursuers.

Fumbling wildly with their flashlights as they scrambled through the tunnels they somehow negotiated the different levels without a problem. When they finally saw daylight, the team outside had heard their yells and the explosions and eager hands reached through the opening they had enlarged to drag them out into the daylight.

Medics quickly went to work on Flowers. When he came to, all he could remember were medics picking shrapnel out of the wounds in his legs. Batman had minor wounds but was okay.

Colonel George Patton the third was standing over Flowers and Batman. His men had found the exit to the tunnel and one of Patton's tanks had the NVAs trapped inside.

Flowers was in no condition to continue pursuit. A medevac helicopter quickly transferred both men to the hospital.

The two Kit Carson men tried to talk the NVA soldiers out of the tunnel without success. So charges were set at both the entrance and the exit and they simultaneously collapsed the entire tunnel system, suffocating the NVA that remained there. (Col. Patton's men later dug up the bodies so they could be added to the body count.)

Both Batman and Flowers had broken eardrums from the grenade explosion. From his hospital bed Flowers said, "If that had been John Wayne he would have picked up that grenade, lifted up that trapdoor and thrown it back at the bastard. If it had been Audie Murphy he would have thrown his body over the grenade to save Batman's life, and his mother would have received his posthumous medal of honor. But since it was Jack Flowers, I crawled so fast I passed my tunnel buddy and somehow we all made it out!"

Bottom line, both men received the Bronze Star (V) from the division's commanding general plus of course Purple Hearts. The Bronze Star is awarded members of the U.S. Armed forces for heroic or meritorious service in a combat zone. The "V" device is for valor.

In the long haul Flowers got his wish of being a hands-on leader and got bloodied in the process. Now he was at least Batman's equal. Once again Batman's charmed luck had rubbed off on them both. Whoever heard of a grenade landing in a guys lap while he's sitting in a pitch-black underground tunnel and somehow he and his buddy escape with their lives? Totally unreal of course but whatever charm was working that day it sure paid off for both of them!

As far as everyone else was concerned they were heroes. Both Flowers and Batman went on to survive the war and made it home in one piece. The elite Diehard Tunnel Rats of The Big Red One would always remember them as the legendary lucky-as-hell Tunnel Rats, Batman and Flowers.

LONE WOLF
OF THE WOLFHOUNDS:
Tunnel Rats of Nam 69

1

One Kind of Lone Wolf

Without realizing it the huge sprawling U.S. Army Base Camp in the Cu Chi district northwest of Saigon was set up atop the largest maze of enemy tunnels ever found in Vietnam.

It was virtually impossible for the Allied Forces with their tunnel rat squads to penetrate and destroy any significant number of the enemy in these miles of tunnels. Even as late as February 1969 the enemy forces, multiplying like a rat infestation in their underground nests, were able to mount successful raids on the American base above them, emerging in the middle of the night from old undiscovered tunnels and using some new ones as well.

Viet Cong prisoners revealed to their interrogators that they had hidden for three to four days directly underfoot before they mounted these successful attacks. This kind of information told them that, at least three years after the arrival of the 25th Infantry Headquarters at this base, they were still not in control of the very ground the base sat upon.

In fact, the base had been described as being a bulky

fortress that was being forced to spend more energy, time and money feeding itself and defending itself. Not a great deal of our knowledge about the way to combat the enemy underground took in the bulk of the scientific information we had learned about the enemy habits there. Our soldiers used the old gung ho tradition of the infantry to fight this scourge. But it all took place above ground. Firefights in the night were not uncommon. They were hit and run; then the enemy disappeared.

A squad was assigned to get down and dirty with the enemy underground but the guys they chose for this super-dangerous job were not too gung ho about the idea. Their sergeant, who was called "The Rock", was purposely chosen for this tough job. His name was Antonio but that got shortened to Tonio. Born to Italian-American parents from Hawaii, he was a short, tough muscular guy with a very stubborn mind-set. There was only one way to do a job and that was the right way. The Rock chose it and he was always right.

Under his leadership this group gradually got its act together. Normally the dangerous job of being a tunnel rat was voluntary. But not as far as The Rock and his squad were concerned. None of them were volunteers. Every one of them was from the elite Wolfhounds, the Second Battalion of the 27th Infantry Regiment of the 25th Division. This outfit began at Fort McPherson, Georgia, in 1901 but it earned its K-9 title and reputation during World War 1. It came about when the White Russians compared the ferocity of this fighting force to that of their giant dog they called a Wolfhound.

If Sergeant Tonio had been with any other outfit in the big Red One dedicated to stamping out the underground enemies, he would have been immediately spotted as one of the most skilled, most determined and most successful of all the tunnel rats. But instead he was with a group that, despite its heritage, never really garnered any fame or recognition from their colleagues. No officers were allowed to go down into those places

When the brass realized the Wolfhounds needed a leader who might be able to salvage their reputation, The Rock was their first choice. They had picked the right man for the job. He already had the reputation of being a lone wolf maverick.

Tonio's mother died when he was a baby. His father, a plantation worker, brought up his three sons. Tonio was the youngest. His older brothers grew up to serve in World War II and then left the service. Tonio's father was a stern man and the boy's early years were hard on him. Yet they also toughened him. His father brought his son up the old-fashioned way believing that if you spared the rod you spoiled the child. His father told him never to back down if he thought that he was right. His father taught him to fight with his fists and never to give up. The boy became so good at it that he became a flyweight boxer. If the youngster did anything that his father thought was wrong, the old man beat him severely.

At the age of nine his father gave him a large knife and told him it was his turn to kill a pig. His father showed him how to do it and admonished him against doing it wrong. Doing it wrong meant getting another painful beating. The old man showed him how to kill with one stroke, telling the boy, "If you fail to do it I'm going to beat the daylights out of you." He told him, "If you ever use a knife in a fight you've gotta be better at it than your opponent or you're dead."

Tonio took this to heart and became extremely proficient at wielding a knife. The boy both loved and feared his father. When he was twenty years old Tonio joined the U.S. Army intending to make a lifetime career of it. Never backing down and refusing to take any order he thought was just plain stupid got him into all kinds of trouble. He spent a lot of time in the stockade. When a superior officer realized how good he was at boxing he was ordered to box for the regiment. Since Tonio had just promised his young wife that he would never box again, he refused to fight for the regiment. The superior officer, who was the colonel making that request, instructed all NCOs to heap all the dirty work they could find on him.

Tonio did the work without complaining and refused to give in. Everyone who knew him knew he wasn't just stubborn to be stubborn. He highly respected discipline and efficiency. After all, those were the qualities his father beat into him all of his young life. He obeyed those he respected. "If a corporal he respected asked him to do something that could cost him his life, he would do it," he said.

When it looked as though a war of wills was escalating between the officer and this stubborn recruit, a close friend suggested that Tonio try a different approach. He suggested that while Tonio couldn't box because of his promise to his wife, he certainly should tell the colonel that he would be willing to be a coach for any other boxer the colonel might have in mind.

This was the perfect solution and in the end Tonio gained the respect of all of them. Everyone who knew him figured that when Tonio became a sergeant his men would look up to him and respect him.

He did and they did. They knew they could count on him because he was solid as a rock, which earned him his nickname.

His superiors saw in Tonio the kind of stuff that made legendary leaders. So with that in mind they gave him the equivalent of "The Dirty Dozen," to work with. They were as negative a bunch of reluctant tunnel rats as you can imagine. They hadn't volunteered, weren't suited, and didn't want any part of that duty. More reason for the brass to see if this sergeant with the calm, cool, steadfast determination of a born leader, could pull it off. Could he turn these misfits into a squad of eager tunnel killers?

While it was a motley group that he had to work with, their leader on the other hand looked as though he had been born to the job. He was built small and compact. All muscle and totally fearless. More bulldog than wolfhound.

While Sergeant Tonio might look as though he was made for the job, some of his squad members didn't. Especially one they all called Tex. He was built like a fullback. The enemy hadn't made a tunnel big enough to accommodate this guy.

Other squad members liked the idea of crawling into those holes in the ground about as much as they liked the idea of being given permanent duty burning shit barrels for the rest of the war.

Sergeant Tonio didn't have the option of handpicking his people for tunnel duty. He had to work with those he had at hand. Fortunately Tonio had managed to persuade their CO, Captain Michael that he be given a free hand to handle this duty as best he could. The captain really didn't want any part in how he did it. He just wanted him to do it on his own terms, the way he felt he could. He didn't want to interfere with them.

The sergeant started out by gathering his squad together and talking to them.

"Listen up, you Wolfhounds," he said. "Thanks to Command's decision, you men have been chosen to be the best and the fiercest tunnel rats you can possibly be, but you aren't going to be doing this alone. Others will be right there with you as backup. And I'll be there too, leading you every step along the way. I promise you that."

At first his men didn't realize that The Rock was not asking for volunteers for this job. He was telling them that this was the job that they were going to do. There were no two ways about it. They had their reputation to live up to and The Rock was going to see that they did.

I'll make the decisions because this has to work perfectly, or it won't work at all."

"I just soon it don't work at all," someone cracked from the rear.

A stunned silence fell over the men. Nobody ever had the guts to question The Rock. They knew better. But one didn't.

It was Tex, the over-sized cowboy. He spoke with a drawl

but his voice was uncommonly high-pitched for such a big man.

Sergeant Tonio worked his way through his men to him. The small sergeant looked up at the big guy and snarled, "I knew that pipsqueak remark didn't come from a Wolfhound," he said. "It came from a Texas wire-haired terrier lap dog."

The big Texan heard his buddies snickering and he bowed up like a cornered Mustang.

"C'mon, Spunky," growled the now crouching little bulldog. "I'll take you on any way you want. Knives or pistols loaded with one round. Take your pick. If you got gripes about the way I run this outfit, I'll be glad to show you what the inside of a body-bag looks like." Talk like that could get a guy a fast trip to a court-martial.

They had heard this kind of threat from The Rock before. Sometimes a knife would be in his right hand. None had ever taken him up on it. All bets were on the little guy being able to do just what he said.

"I ain't goin' in no tunnel," muttered Tex. "Y'all can take that to the bank." He directed this loud remark to the guys who had snickered.

Rock unclenched his fists as he grinned and turned away from the cowboy. "If we need you down in those tunnels brother, we'll just whittle you to size."

That got a burst of laughter from the onlookers, relieved the tension was gone. As usual The Rock never budged. But Tonio knew from that moment on the big Texan was trouble. Sooner or later the two of them would tangle.

Sergeant Tonio used his challenge frequently whenever the squad disagreed with his tactics. No one ever took him up on it because they all knew how bad it would end for everyone.

Of course all of this was the kind of thing the sergeant could be court-martialed for if anyone complained to a higher authority. But no one did. So, slowly but surely The Rock's team of would-be tunnel rats began to shape up for this dangerous role.

One of the squad members even smaller than The Rock whose nickname was Gangsta because he was from Chicago, usually was their point man. The Rock made sure that no one went entirely alone into this dangerous place. They all adopted the standard equipment and procedures of the successful tunnel rats. At the time that procedure included staying in radio contact with surface troops so that both sides knew what was going on. There was nothing wireless about this operation. The rats dragged a lot of telephone cable along with them on their search and destroy missions.

The Rock hammered into them the importance of being constantly vigilant – to look at every detail and consider them potential booby-traps. Soon the entire squad began to shape up as a workable group of rats, even with Tex. It wasn't that he was a bad soldier or a screw-up but he was just too big for this kind of duty.

Because of his robust size he was their heavy machine-gun man. His broad shoulders could easily carry the load. But there was no place for a machine-gun in the tunnels. So his job now was mainly to stand outside the entrance and guard it. He not only didn't mind this duty but he even began to take pride in it. He was there to pass supplies to the guys underground or to haul on a rope to bring out captives or the wounded. Mainly too, The Rock told him to chase away any friendly troops who might be in the area. No one wanted guys with itchy trigger fingers going off half-cocked when they suddenly saw a grimy-faced rat pop out of a hole near them.

On one occasion the squad was sent out on an overnight patrol. Everything went smoothly. The guards were posted and the rest turned in. In the middle of the night Sergeant Tonio awakened to check the guards. He found Tex asleep at his post.

This was a major court-martial offense. The sergeant took the husky Texan's M-14 rifle away from him. As he did, Tex woke up, grabbed his bayonet and attacked Tonio. Instantly the sergeant pulled out his knife and the two fought each other. In a flash the sergeant's knife cut Tex's neck.

At first light Sergeant Tonio ordered the private to make a formal report of the incident to their Company Commander, Captain Michael. Both men had committed serious offenses and could be subject to court-martial.

While Tex made his way to the commander's quarters to report the incident, Sergeant Tonio called his CO on the company field phone and told him what happened.

Captain Michael listened to Tex's report of the event. Then he chewed him out from one end to the other for the next half hour emphasizing that the enemy could have overrun their entire platoon because of his carelessness … an act that in other wars was punishable by the culprit facing a firing squad on the spot. But this time, thanks to Sergeant Tonio asking him not to report the incident, he wouldn't. But the commander let Tex know that he was damn lucky to escape with his life because Tonio could have killed him on the spot. That was the end of the incident.

But it surely wasn't the end of the tension between the two men. The Rock saw Tex as a weak link in their platoon. He somehow had to remedy it, or get rid of the problem.

Shortly after that the platoon was transferred to bunkers near the base perimeter. They were now close enough to the surrounding jungle that Viet Cong snipers were always taking pot shots at the men.

So far no one had been hit but it was extremely bothersome because sooner or later one of the brothers would be killed. So Sergeant Tonio focused his attention on this problem. He noted when and how often the sniper fired on them and from which direction it most often occurred.

It seemed that it came from a tree well within their base perimeter. But that made no sense at all because our forces surrounded the tree. He could not figure how the sniper was getting into it, taking his shot, and escaping. Every time it happened the machine gunners blanketed that area with hot lead. All that did was shred the rubber plantation trees in the background.

No matter what they did, nothing prevented that elusive sniper from firing on them the very next day!

Finally, the frustrated sergeant set up machine guns to fire specifically at the top and at the bottom of that tree the next time the sniper took a pot shot at them. And to tempt the shooter into action, the sergeant ordered the one man he could spare – Tex to walk past that tree especially just before lunch time when it seemed the sniper most often fired.

The sergeant said, "Walk briskly but don't stop, because if you stop you're liable to take a round from this guy. The minute he fires we're going to be on him."

Tex long ago gave up arguing with The Rock. One thing he didn't plan to do was take his time making that walk. The only thing he had going for him was that the sniper so far couldn't hit the broad side of a barn. Still … he thought, *this time he might!*

Of course what the sergeant asked him to do was a court-martial offense, but what else was new? If Tex lived and made the report, the higher ups would just congratulate him on living through it. And if he didn't … well it made no difference, did it? Tex clenched his teeth and psyched himself up for the ordeal.

The machine-gunners were zeroed in and ready. The time was right … just before lunch. From around the corner of a sand-bagged bunker The Rock signaled and the tall hulking form of the Texas cowboy moved at a rather fast pace from between the bunkers on a straight shot to the mess hall.

Suddenly from the tree 100 meters to his left an AK-47 cracked out loud and clear. Tex dropped like a sandbag.

A pair of M-60 machine-guns peppered the sniper's tree.

In a couple swift bounds Sergeant Tonio raced to the crumpled figure of Tex. Instantly he regretted what he had done. Overcome with remorse his eyes swept the big guy's form. Where was he hit?

Suddenly, Tex's eyes popped open, "**Did you get him**?"

Tonio's heart leaped in relief when he saw Tex wasn't wounded; *he had fainted!*

Rock patted his shoulder. "Not yet, Pal, but you did good." The two actually grinned at each other.

Half the guys heading for chow that day ganged up at the shot-to-hell sniper's tree expecting to see the bullet-riddled remains of the shooter on the ground beside it.

But no such sight met their eyes. Now, however, the bullet-riddled tree revealed its secret. It was dead and it was hollow. A long rope hung down inside it to a tunnel underground. That's how the sniper came and went. The shooter was long gone and soon so was that tree.

After that incident, Tex humbly asked Sergeant Tonio if he would please not use him as sniper bait anymore. Smiling, The Rock shook hands with him and said he wouldn't. From then on Tex went back to his best-liked job of guarding tunnel entrances while the team explored them. But now he did it with a certain new sense of pride. The vendetta between the two men was over. Both had gained a hard-earned new respect for the other. Both were solid brothers at arms now. The pride of the Wolfhounds was back and shared by one and all.

The Rock put the tunnel rat crew through their paces so often that they became a well-oiled operation. He was always there to help them, as were the others. They never went down into a tunnel without a backup system. Tex took on his tunnel entrance guard duty with gusto. He knew the guys didn't want the team to come boiling out of one of those holes and have friendlies think they were the enemy and take them out. They all let him know how much they counted on him there too. He was a major part of the team and would never let them down.

The 25th Infantry's search and destroy tunnel operations, that ran for seven months, located 577 tunnels in the Cu Chi area alone. But of all the reports that were generated few of them even mentioned the importance of the tunnel rats. And beside the Wolfhounds, there were many other Tunnel Rat operations involved as well.

Despite the rule that officers were never to go down into the tunnels, that certainly didn't keep them out of there if they so chose that kind of action.

Sergeant Tonio's men became trim and fit for the operation. Each man knew his job and he did it well. The Rock had trained them to work as a team; to support each other. This support kept them safe from blundering into hidden booby traps or the VC lying in wait for them in the dark.

They were a very disciplined group, the kind of discipline that had been beat into their sergeant many years ago. Now it kept them safe from harm. Tonio may have been a lone wolf in his principles but it was teamwork that he was most proud of because it worked. Never less than three men went into a tunnel. The men worked together the same way a pack of wolves work together to take down their prey. The full tunnel rat team making a extended exploration of the system was never less than five men. More often, six. Two were assigned the tunnel entrance, both to guard against friendlies but also to pass supplies forward or to help recover a rat in trouble as swiftly as possible.

The group's point man as usual was the lone wolf himself. And he was never less than five meters ahead of the number two man behind him. The reason for that was the second man would not be taken out by an accidental tripping of a booby trap by the point man.

If a tunnel split and went off in another direction, one man remained there to direct the others behind him, in case they were being led into a trap, or that it was a false dead end.

Whenever trap doors were discovered they were dynamited, rather than blown up by grenades because the dynamite did not take up so much oxygen as a grenade would.

The Rock stuck with the basic equipment. None of the

fancy stuff that was being issued now for tunnel rats. A pistol, the communication wire and a flashlight was it because it worked for them.

If the tunnel rats found other entrances leading to the surface they were careful about checking them out in case friendlies reacted as you might expect whenever a grimy soldier popped out of the ground near them. It was common at that time for tunnel rats to carry a red light for such occasions because the VC certainly did not use them. But neither did The Rock's group. They avoided contact with our troops entirely.

Some tunnel rat groups felt that the more noise they made the better it would be. The enemy would hear them coming and would leave the premises as quickly as possible. Others entered the tunnels as quietly as they could, intending hopefully to surprise the guerrillas.

True to his word Sergeant Tonio developed what he called "a buddy system" as a way to explore the tunnels in their area safely. Nobody went into the tunnels alone. Nobody crawled so far ahead that he and the person behind him lacked protection for each other.

The sergeant drilled them on their performance and it worked like clockwork. The squad was totally synchronized and because of their buddy system not one of the sergeant's tunnel rats was even wounded. The group was as proud of their performance as was Sergeant Tonio. They developed a reputation in the base for efficiency as being one finely tuned group of tunnel rats.

In the course of these missions they discovered underground conference rooms, whose walls were bedecked with Hammer and Sickle flags of the Communist Party. They often found large stores of rice, weapons, and important documents. Rather than use the red flashlight system to identify themselves to the friendlies, the sergeant cleared away all friendlies in the area of their tunnel explorations so there would be no question that they were alone.

When any other friendlies came into their sacred area The Rock drove them off. If anyone argued with him he was ready to take him on in his usual hand-to-hand encounters. No one did.

Eventually, all of the men making up the sergeant's group of tunnel rats were wounded in firefights but not in any underground skirmish. It all happened above ground.

Sergeant Tonio had been reported so many times for his unethical manner of training that his superiors expected it. They all knew that he got results, so they looked the other way.

Sergeant Tonio kept the agreement he made with his men. Thanks to his training they not only survived all their missions underground, but they once again earned the respect of their comrades for their reputation as Wolfhounds. Sergeant Tonio was indeed the leader of men his superiors knew he was. Though he was still a lone wolf and a maverick, in recognition of what he had achieved the military awarded him two Silver Stars, three Bronze Stars, and the Army Commendation Medal.

After his success as lone wolf of the wolfhounds, The Rock was transferred from the 25th Infantry and Cu Chi to where the military figured there was a more demanding need for his maverick skills. He became a U.S. Advisor to ARVN, the Army of the Republic of Vietnam. These South Vietnamese soldiers trained as our support troops. After that The Rock was assigned to Korea but the lack of action there bored him. When Sergeant Tonio left the service he ended up in Hawaii, working as a civilian next to our huge army base there.

2

Another Kind of Lone Wolf

Every war has them. Sergeant Tonio was one kind of lone wolf sometimes found in the types that became tunnel rats. There were others. In Nam a young Cuban-American who came from a different background would not have been surprised to know how much that background contributed to the kind of tunnel rat he was. Staff Sergeant Juan Ortega was another kind of lone wolf. And believe me, he was a totally unique one! His buddies always wanted to be close to him, praying that whatever he had would rub off on them. And no matter how you look at it, no one can explain what caused his situation unless you want to consider it divine intervention. Here's how it went:

Sergeant Juan Ortega was known for his bravery and incredibly good luck. Juan liked nothing better than taking out the Commies. He was a Commie killer. He got that way from Day One. By the time he found his way to being point man for one dedicated group of tunnel rats, no one would believe it because he just wasn't built to be one!

This Cuban-American was lanky and almost 6 feet tall. Not short and muscular as most rats were. As a teenager he grew up in Havana when Fidel Castro's revolutionaries were in the process of getting rid of dictator Batista's regime. Ortega's teenage pastime in those days was to borrow his father's .38 and take pot shots at Castro's communist revolutionaries. Surprisingly the youngster lived to make it to Florida. He chose to earn his American citizenship by joining the U.S. Army, fighting what he was told were the communists infiltrating South Vietnam.

Incredibly, his good luck followed him there. He used it in mine detecting on Vietnam's Highway 13 in 1968. Private Ortega was the first to discover that the enemy mines and grenade booby traps were actually homemade. The enemy was using found or stolen American explosives and turning them against us in the most devastating ways.

Speaking of good luck, on three … count them … three different occasions, Juan Ortega was possibly the only living soldier who heard the sound made by stepping on a mine and the sound of it being sprung … yet for some reason it did not go off!

Three times!

And each time after it happened Juan checked out the mine and found it in perfect working order!

Juan's buddies were a close group. He may not have noticed it but others did. Whenever they went into combat together his buddies had a habit of sticking close to him. They may have figured he had some kind of arrangement with the Man upstairs and they hoped whatever it was might rub off on them as well.

Who knows? Sergeant Ortega certainly seemed to live a charmed life in Nam.

Gifted might be a word for it. Whatever it was, Juan had it. Those who knew him swore that he could even sniff out a mine. The minesweepers could go through an area and swear that it was clean. Along came Juan, his nostrils twitching, only to declare that it wasn't clean. And right beside them he would dig up a live mine.

Whatever it was that attracted this lanky Cuban-American to sniff out mines and even tread on them without losing his life may have been one of the strong impulses that brought him to become an exceptional tunnel rat.

He had the killer instinct. He typified the lone wolf that eagerly sought to kill all communists he could find.

He would spend three years in Vietnam, two years longer

than necessary. Three years tracking danger and death so closely that he almost believed the obscene idea that he alone could face death and would always survive it.

No matter how it came to be so important to him, whether it was from his early teens in Cuba, the fight for freedom to be an American citizen, or just for the glory of our flag, he was a natural-borne killer with a Guardian Angel in armor sitting on his shoulder!

In the tunnels he never took prisoners. He was addicted to the adrenaline highs that sharpened his reflexes and his ability to see, smell, and react to any challenge. This was his special arena. He was underground hunting and killing commies. Whenever he was there in the sweaty, stench-filled dark, feeling more wolf that human, with superhuman senses working for him, he was at his best and seldom returned without making a kill. Man hunting man. The ultimate high. He couldn't get enough of it.

Surely he considered himself invincible. He loved the idea of the enemy rats crawling out of their holes to attack the Americans in the dead of night; then scurrying back into their holes trying to escape. Let the cat and rat games begin! Hard on their trail came the commie-hunters with Juan leading the way. If the enemy went deep, Juan and his men followed. Everyone was hyped on adrenaline. Lights out the pursuers followed at a quickened pace that leader Ortega had taught them. Elbows and knees going at high speed that took the skin off all areas. But not after he repeatedly drilled them in "Ortega's Crawl." They didn't even feel it now thanks to their thick calluses. But boy they moved fast. Nobody worried about booby traps here because the enemy was ahead of them scrambling to escape. Right behind them, wriggling like digging ferrets, came the hungry pack of swift pursuers.

Sooner or later the cats caught the rats and the pursuit was all over but for the shooting. No prisoners were ever brought out. No body count ever made. The lanky almost six foot tall Sergeant Ortega who boasted that he could turn around in any tunnel ever built did exactly that. And so too could each of his rats. Three of them in a line coming back at high speed through those tunnels must have looked like a very long squirming giant millipede.

If for any reason he was assigned a mission in a hotspot and had already psyched himself up to the point that it took, Sergeant Ortega almost freaked out if the mission was called off for some reason. The tremendous letdown made him so sick to his stomach that he often heaved ... because he couldn't go after the detested enemy and kill them.

You didn't need to be a psychiatrist to know that this gifted hunter, who took on the chore of point man more times than he was actually allowed, was addicted to this blood sport. This skinny tall fellow who stepped on mines and lived had a double personality. When he went into these endless burrows, his personality changed and he became the lone wolf of legend, calculating and crafty, fangs dripping, hyped to make his kill. His men knew it. So did his superiors. In the end they heaped words of praise on him and gave him medals for his bravery.

The citation that went with Sergeant Juan Ortega's Commendation Medal (V) was a resounding tribute to the man's bravery. It described this gifted tunnel rat who, despite all odds, swiftly entered a tunnel that was already a death trap because the enemy had wounded two of his squad there. And it was Juan Ortega who quickly volunteered to search this tunnel for documents and then destroy it.

"He then entered this hot hole," said the citation, "that had already been contaminated with CS gas and refused to wear a gas mask without any concern for his own safety. Then he crawled deeper into this tunnel with the explosives that were to destroy it." But what the official document does not mention is the fact that Juan knew there was a hidden enemy soldier in that tunnel. A North Vietnam Army soldier lay in wait for him there.

Despite the choking fumes of the gas, Juan had smelled

the enemy. The same way he had smelled out their mines. He was like a wolf following a blood spoor. He had refused the gas mask because it would have blocked his ability to smell the enemy.

In one part of that tunnel he got stuck because it simply was too small for him. So he got out his knife and was widening the opening when all of a sudden an enemy soldier appeared in front of him. He was not a Viet Cong but a North Vietnamese Army soldier in a dull green uniform. He carried an AK-47.

No one will ever know why the soldier did not instantly shoot the tunnel rat that was already stuck in the tunnel. Juan did not fire because he had been ordered to bring back any prisoners that he found. Well he had found one. But he sure didn't have the drop on him!

Despite the narrow constriction of the tunnel this lanky tunnel rat flipped around and did a fast crawl retreat to the tunnel entrance. How he managed that without taking a slug in the back from the soldier's AK-47 no one can even guess. Maybe the soldier was so shocked by their meeting that all he wanted to do was disappear as fast as he could in the opposite direction.

In any case Juan never told his men that there was an NVA soldier down there with him. All he asked for was a shaped charge. He was going back there to blow the tunnel.

His companions gave him a forty-pound cratering charge of C-4 and this gung-ho commie killer crawled all the way back in search of the enemy soldier he had left there.

When he arrived at the spot his flashlight did not reveal the man but Juan's nostrils told him he was still there. He smelled the fishy sweat and body odor.

Later Juan recalled wondering if once the charge went off how many of the enemy would be killed when the tunnel caved in. Again he swiftly exited using his elbows and knees to claw his way back to the entrance.

When the explosion came it was like kicking the roof off a

large fire ant mound to expose a maze of new tunnels. According to the citation it was Sergeant Juan Ortega who wanted to be the first to go down into those tunnels after the blast to see how many commies he had killed.

They prevented him going only by dangling a carrot on a stick before his eyes. The carrot was an order to report to Guam for ten days so he could receive his hard-earned tribute of becoming an American citizen, something he had dreamed about ever since leaving Cuba.

Obviously this gifted lone wolf would gladly have stayed down in the tunnels of Vietnam forever if he could. But to his disappointment the war was winding down and this wolf was headed toward another way of life.

He realized that truth when the military told him that he had given all that he could give to the war effort and it was now time for him to take his hard-won medals and U.S. citizenship and go home. Which is what he reluctantly did. But the highs of the life he led in Nam he never could leave behind. Back in the States he got married and divorced three times. He never talked about his days in the tunnels. Nor did he attend any veteran's reunions. He did buy an arsenal of weapons, moved to Colorado and began hunting big game with a vengeance. Like all lone wolves in retirement, Juan Ortega always hunts alone.

TUNNEL SECRETS OF VIETNAM
And What We Found There!

1

The Enemy Underfoot

During the Vietnam War we had no idea how large and complex were their secret underground tunnel systems. But in time we found out. We learned that the underground tunnels of Cu Chi were part of a major network that when the war was at its worst in the mid 1960s these tunnels stretched from Saigon to the border of Cambodia, encompassing hundreds of kilometers of tunnels so vast that they connected villages, districts and providences in larger numbers than any surface highways. There were living quarters, vast storage areas, factories that made ordinance, hospitals that treated the wounded, headquarters where enemy leaders worked out complex attacks against us and almost any other facilities you can think of that supported the war and provided hideouts virtually beyond the reach of our all-encompassing air force attacks.

After the war General Westmoreland, commander of the American forces in Vietnam from 1964 to 1968, said in his memoirs:

"No one has ever demonstrated more ability to hide his installations than the Viet Cong. They were human moles."

Early in the war no one had even scratched the surface to the secret underground system. That's not to say that we didn't try with the very best tunnel rats we had available at the time. None of them were more qualified for this kind of operation than one man who had all the physical qualifications necessary: he was short, thin and he had the instincts of a fighting bulldog. This then is a fictional account of his experiences in those tunnels, all based on facts that often were not available to us until after the war. This scenario was certainly familiar to many of the soldiers fighting the Vietnam War in the early years.

It was a rubber plantation on the edge of a landing zone that was beginning to look like a scene from World War II. The Americans had set up a tight defensive perimeter but they were suffering casualties that were strangely and alarmingly increasing, apparently from random attacks by the Viet Cong.

It seemed to our troops that the enemy could appear and disappear like magic. All along the northern edge of the landing zone the men were well dug in. These experienced combat troops were fully aware that the enemy was also dug in – but not one of our boys figured that they might actually be underfoot. The GIs quickly shut down any holes they found that might be connected to these tunnels.

They found one that was obviously man-made for Vietnamese-sized troops because it was no more than a foot in diameter. It angled downward at about forty-five degrees. In truth, what they had really stumbled on was a tunnel's ventilation hole.

At chow that evening the troops were settling down for the night when they abruptly heard several sharp grenade explosions followed by carbine shots. But what really grabbed their attention was that all of this was coming from *within their own perimeter*! When an officer ran over to the area where the grenades had gone off the first thing he saw were GIs standing around a small hole in the ground.

One of the men said, "We were just sitting around yakking when all of a sudden the ground right in front of us opens up and this frickin' little guy jumps out and throws two grenades. Then he reaches down, grabs a carbine and sprays us. Before any of us know what to do, Charlie jumps back into his little hole, slams the trapdoor and he's gone!"

2

Get Shorty!

Fortunately, one of our best tunnel rats named Shorty was with a patrol not far away and he quickly went down to see what he could find. When he didn't return for the next two-and-a-half hours everyone topside figured the worst had happened. They were putting together a rescue mission into the widened tunnel mouth when Shorty suddenly popped up again looking like he had been crawling through mud. Only the round whites of his eyes told the GIs he was one of them.

He told them that he had gone at least a mile and a half underground; most of it in the dark; feeling with his hands for any bad news the little guy might have left behind for him.

Once he found nothing he stepped up his pace, using his penlight only for seconds to orient himself to tunnel changes. He didn't want to miss any side-door escape routes so his hands became his eyes. He probably looked like a crazy orchestra leader waving his arms in every direction. But his fingers fluttered carefully, sending information about what they touched back to his brain for instant analysis as to whether it was safe or not safe. His hands moved swiftly over the bottom then up the walls and overhead like large white spiders always feeling things and letting Shorty know it was safe to squirm on ahead as fast as he dared go considering the circumstances. He might be a blind mole, but all of his other senses were working overtime.

He guessed most likely there was no one ahead of him. His advantage was being able go to twice as fast as his pursuer, literally scampering off to wherever fleeing rats go when they make a high speed escape.

Later, follow-up tunnel rats checking Shorty's tunnel again found several large underground side chambers but they were all empty. The squad had already enlarged the tunnel opening and this time went down with their field telephones, gas grenades, gas masks, flashlights, handguns and compasses.

Shorty's group of trained tunnel rats were now able to communicate with their topside counterparts following their progress underground so they had some idea of what was happening down there.

Carefully the rats explored details of the passageways, going swiftly along tunnels that Shorty had already scouted. There was no problem.

These tunnels were too heavily used by the Viet Cong to bother setting mines. The searchers followed the tunnel for a mile and a quarter when the underground rats saw a light ahead.

Through their communication setup, the topside troops heard what were the first recorded sounds of underground firefight between Americans and the Viet Cong. The tunnel rats pulled on their gas masks and threw gas grenades at the enemy. The noisy encounter didn't last long. In all the smoke, gas and confusion the enemy disappeared through a number of concealed escape routes.

The next morning Shorty was point man for another search. Their commander ordered the tunnels to be carefully and closely explored. This thoroughness resulted in them finding a basket of grenades that covered a secret trap door to a second level. Carefully they made their way down to this tunnel and were amazed to find rooms filled with sacks of rice and stacks of weapons.

3

They Recycled Our Trash

Not far away another company's tunnel rats discovered the opening to a secret tunnel complex where no one would have thought to look for a tunnel opening. It was in an anthill! They found it when an enemy soldier suddenly jumped out of it; shot an American and then dived back into his hole again. When the GIs rushed the anthill they discovered the secret entrance just behind it.

Back at the main area that the military was now calling the Ho Bo Woods, one of the tunnel rats discovered a diary written by a Viet Cong soldier. It translated later to read:

"Have spent four days in tunnel. About 8 to 9 thousand American soldiers were in for a sweep operation. The attack was fierce in the last few days. A number of underground tunnels collapsed. Some of our men were caught in them and have not been able to get out yet. It is not known what has become of sisters (he gave three names) in these tunnels. In an attempt to provide security he gave the name of two Viet Cong that were killed, and added that their bodies left unattended deteriorated, [and] have not been buried yet.

In the afternoon one of our village unit members trying to stay close to the enemy for reconnaissance was killed and his body has not been recovered.

Fifteen minutes ago enemy jets dropped bomb; houses collapsed and trees fell. I was talking when a rocket exploded two meters away and bombs poured down like a torrent. We should fight them, we should kill them, you [U. S. soldiers] will have no way out. It is always dark before sunrise. After cold days warm days will come. The most tiresome moment comes when one moves up a hill one must raise up disregarding death and hardships, determined to fight the American aggressors.

On hard days, one has to stay in [the] tunnels, eat cold rice with salt, and drink uncooked water. However one is free and feels at ease." This entry was written in January 1966.

This diary was one of 8,000 items the Americans captured in those tunnels. While some of the tunnels were obviously in such heavy use they were not mined, tunnels in other areas of this huge complex were just the opposite. Outside the tunnels, around the entrance areas, troops found homemade grenades rigged as anti-personal mines with trip wires strung from trees ranging from ankle height to head height.

Another group found two mortar bombs triggered by a grenade that could be set off by an ankle high trip wire. Other tunnels contained razor-sharp bamboo stakes set in concrete. One of the men attached to an Aussi sapper company of militia accidentally stepped on one and it went straight through his foot.

As one tunnel system was being searched by GIs a firefight broke out. Not only were they killed but so were the medical evacuation people that came to their aid. Troops immediately rushed to this hotspot and surrounded it, but when they tightened this noose they could not find a single enemy soldier. They had all vanished down escape routes in the tunnels.

In the following days the tunnel explorers found at least three-quarters of a mile of communication tunnels, a number of bunkers and underground chambers. Enough to tell them that this was a very complex and extensive underground system.

In an effort to understand where and how far it stretched they came up with the idea of using a powerful blower system that would pump smoke into the underground chambers with the hope that watching at the surface they could see it coming out of hitherto hidden airways and entranceways. What sounded like a good idea went bad when the smoke simply disappeared into the tunnels, and took all the oxygen out of the air underground. When soldiers went in trying to explore these intricate corridors they immediately had problems because they couldn't breathe in them. One Australian tunnel rat got caught in one of the underground trapdoors and before his comrades could dig him out he lost his life from asphyxiation.

The first things that were done in these smoked areas was to set up the blower to blow fresh air down into the chambers and get rid of the smoke. Behind them came the diligent tunnel ferrets [as the Aussies called themselves] trying to explore these amazing mazes. These brave men found large storage areas of ammunition.

Once they came up with a system of communication with their surface people it worked well. Those on top could follow the progress with those underground, but there was no end to all the surprises they found hidden in those secret rooms.

In one place the room was filled with sewing machines! What the underground workers produced there were flags! It was a flag-making factory in the dark except for the bottle lamps of vegetable oil they all carried. Incredible! No electric sewing machines here. They all were manually pedaled. Though the data doesn't say who did the pedaling one could guess that this was where a lot of Vietnamese women did their part for the war effort.

In other underground chambers were storage areas for large caches of rice, the kind of food the enemy could live on indefinitely as long as they had this resource. What surprised the underground explorers however was discovering that these rooms were not only mined but sometimes had hidden booby traps within the bagsful of rice!

There was no end to this surprising cleverness the enemy showed by taking advantage even of American trash the troops left behind. This became evident when the tunnel rats uncovered a workshop where the diligent enemy fashioned homemade hand grenades. What surprised them was finding that the inner casing for these was a throwaway tomato juice can. The outer casing was an old beer can. The fragmentation pieces were discarded sharpened pieces of blue metal road rubble and the thing that set all of this off was a firing mechanism from an old French or American grenade! Nothing couldn't be re-used by these clever people.

Considering how all of this trash was being turned into deadly weapons against us by this underground army, what could be done about it? We quickly initiated a policy called, "Burn – Bury."

To keep these materials from being used against us in their recycled form of deadly weapons, the troops were told to burn, smash or bury those items. For example they had 24-hour food rations put up in small tins. The policy now was to never ever leave that tin around to be found by the enemy and used against us.

4

Secrets We Learned

Early on American GIs were learning about the tunnels the hard way. Just before the end of Operation Crimp they brought a mechanized flame-thrower to support the infantry attacking the Viet Cong north of Ho Bo woods. It was used to burn away jungle growth near trenches and around tunnel entrances many of which in this area had trap doors that linked them to either escape routes or other tunnels below the one being explored.

One of the flame thrower operators said, "We started going down checking tunnels out, and right in the middle of it, while we were going into one tunnel they [the VC] would pop up on the surface somewhere else and the shooting would be going on up above you. You could hear them above ground shooting and you never knew if you popped up out of one of those holes whether somebody from our side might take a shot at you. So you tried to tell the guys – in them days we didn't lay wire or nothing because we were working blind – we use to tell them to hold off if they saw us coming out from a different hole to the one that we went in. Hell, you didn't know where you were going to come out.

"I went down there, I got real close to Charlie – [found his] warm food; papers lying around, even found a calendar with the day's date on it, now that's pretty damn close. But the truth is, I'd rather run them out, than meet them down there."

This soldier got pretty well informed about tunnel warfare. He made drawings of what he found including the water traps. These, it turned out, were not intended as rain drainage systems in the tunnels as we once thought. Their real purpose was to prevent tear gas attacks. These water pools found in a descending tunnel blocked the way of underground explorers. These sumps were allowed to fill up with the filthiest water imaginable by the VC not only to stop intruders but mainly to stop gas attacks from going any further into their tunnel system. The enemy simply ducked underwater and swam a short distance to emerge in a tunnel with fresh air coming in through their numerous cleverly hidden ventilation ducts.

How we learned this secret is not known but I suspect one of the captured VC revealed it to us. The first tunnel explorers who found these pools of water blocking their way may have checked them out the hard way. They waded in, held their breath and swam deeper into the tunnel, always believing that they could do it on one lungful of air. Of course no one knew what awaited them on the other side. It took an extremely brave soldier to go this route never knowing if where they came out the enemy would be waiting in the darkness to take them out. Also, you never knew whether there was a way to escape this water trap, which you can imagine, was about as clean as that found in a sewer. You came out of it with a stench about you that lasted for days.

5

Why Operation Crimp Failed

Operation Crimp barely scratched the surface of what it was intended to do mainly because no one really understood what an incredibly complex and extensive underground system the Vietnamese had dug for themselves over the years. Here's how one of our officer's described our enemy, those incredible men in the tunnels:

"They were extremely dedicated guerillas whose lives were totally different from those westerners they were fighting. They learned to live a sparse existence in the world of these tunnels. They wore the kind of clothes often seen by the Vietnamese peasant workers – more often than not what we described as black silk pajamas. This was their uniform and they were the same clothes of the non-combatant peasants. They never wore any badge of rank but a checkered scarf was known always as the badge of the guerilla. On their feet was what was called Ho Chi Minh sandals. They were cut from the tread portion of truck tires with a piece of rubber inner-tube attached that went between the big toe and the second toe the way our flip-flops do. These fighters carried only the essentials required for their existence. This included a tightly rolled hammock often made of U.S. parachute nylon. Another piece of this material wrapped their daily rice ration the size of a snowball. When possible they added sun-dried small fish to the rice. They carried a Chinese-made canteen of water and a homemade lamp often made from a small medicine bottle filled with vegetable oil for lighting their way in the pitch-black tunnels they crawled through. Some of these tunnel guerillas we knew practiced a habit of remaining hidden underground during the daylight hours and emerging at night to attack our forces that were usually asleep. Many of these underground fighters were found wearing leather wrist straps so comrades could drag them more easily into a tunnel if they were wounded or killed."

Operation Crimp was supposed to solve the tunnel problem. Tunnels we found were blown up or contaminated with CS-1 powder. This poison was to contaminate the tunnels so that they would never be used again.

But what we failed to consider was that many tunnels had hard-to-open trap doors and water traps that kept these tunnels from being contaminated.

Most of the military felt Crimp was a success that would end the problem of the tunnels, which was only partially true. As one long-time professional officer in the Vietnamese People's Army said, "Nothing was lost that couldn't be replaced."

He claimed that the 'Viet Cong had survived mainly because they were highly mobile and used flexible structures capable of standing up against the short, drastic American hammer blows so that they could re-emerge fighting." He was right.

The reason that Operation Crimp failed was because it had not destroyed the enemy's infrastructure. It only pointed out the weakness of our search and destroy tactics that were to become normal procedure for the U.S. Army.

The only thing Operation Crimp revealed was the enormous complex that honeycombed the Cu Chi area. Contrary to our propaganda, the United States military was not facing a bunch of Communist terrorists that were infiltrating from the north to a quiet South Vietnamese peasant country that was being held hostage.

Instead, we found a highly trained, dedicated new enemy that was much better armed and organized that we had imagined. One that was extremely clever in all of its underground manifestations. That enemy could choose its own conditions of combat and through their incredibly large subterranean tunnel system they were able to operate wherever and whenever they chose. For the first time we became aware of the real Viet Cong.

6

The Upgraded Enemy

Early in the war the enemy's weapons and equipment were extremely poor. It was either something that had been stolen, or was improvised or homemade. That was the situation up until 1966 when Chinese-made assault rifles – the AK-47 – reached them either by the Ho Chi Minh Trail or by the sea through Cambodia. This weapon became standard for them. Their officers usually carried a Polish K-54 pistol.

Since this enemy lacked air power or artillery, which our Allied Forces relied upon, they in turn used guerrilla tactics on the jungle trails using hidden mines and booby traps. To avoid our air force and artillery, they resorted to ambushes and middle-of-the–night hit-and-run tactics. They called it "grabbing the enemy by the belt," and fighting hand-to-hand, preventing us using air strikes or artillery barrages that would take out our own troops.

If they couldn't win the war at least they could stalemate it. Those were the tactics against which we fought so hard. Most GIs had only a general idea of what we were fighting for in this war. Most saw it as a way of stopping the incursion of communism that was coming in from North Vietnam to South Vietnam. We were there trying to stem that flow.

But the Viet Cong were fighting for other reasons. This was their country and their land to which they so closely bonded. Mother Earth herself became their protection. And it was Mother Earth that they clung to, digging their tunnels under their villages and their ancestral fields.

The tunnels hid the guerillas from the searching soldiers

and from the bombs and the shells. Within those tunnels were the muscles and nerve system of their vast war machine – in the very place where no one would suspect it! Right under our boots were their munitions factories, their food supplies, their armory of stashed arms, their hospitals, their places where their troops lay in wait for their nighttime attacks when we were sleeping; and of course there too were their headquarters, the very heart of their war machine – everything we had to capture if we were to win. We never learned the tremendous importance of all of this until after the war.

7

The Tunnels' Biggest Secret

As I've described in other books about these tunnels it can not be emphasized enough that the builders were well aware that the tunnels had to be built with strict dimensions because part of their clever thinking was that if a tunnel is customized to fit only a certain-sized person then all others would be unable to go there. They had automatically kept the larger-framed western soldier out of them, which made pursuit impossible.

But far the biggest secret of the entire tunnel system was their belief that any pursuers that could follow them and destroy the tunnels would believe that there was just one level of tunnel to be concerned with. Which of course was true. We thought once we cleared it out and blew it up, that was the end of the tunnel threat.

What we didn't know was that they had already expected this and had built hidden trap doors that led to tunnels on different levels, as many as three levels deep. All of those levels with the accompanying systems to keep them properly ventilated and supplied with the necessities of life by the people who would spend up to several years living in them underground!

These tunnels were started sometime in the 1940s for different reasons and digging was carried right on through the years, expanding their complexities through the Indochinese wars with the French up into 1965 and onward. Over all those years the tunnel builders simply improved, expanded, and increased these secret hidden structures. All of them were designed purposely to avoid any long-term fighting in them.

Not only were they built to required dimensions but also none of them went straight very far in any one direction. None of them were allowed the curves of a snake for example. Instead they were built to zigzag with sharp angles. This was done to prevent anyone shooting very far in a straight line. Also it blocked the force of explosions and held back gas attacks. Especially where trap doors were in place to shut off portions of the tunnel in the same manner as the water traps. Any tunnel fighter simply made their way to hidden trap doors that led them to another level of tunnels or offered them an escape route far from the one being hammered by our soldiers.

All of these things were well thought out by the clever minds that had designed this complex underground maze. Everything had to be worked out. The complex ventilating system, the sanitation system, the methods of cooking underground without drawing attention; how to provide light to this perpetual darkness when needed; how to live like a mole in this insect-ridden environment without going stark raving mad.

Life as they knew it continued as normal as possible. People got married underground; entertainers in groups moved through the intricate passageways and put on stage shows and performances for the underground inhabitants. When our troops retired to their barbed-wire encampments, the enemy bided their time sleeping off the sunlit hours so they could be fresh to emerge and have a firefight with the Americans after dark. One wonders if any GI ever heard eerie music coming from right under his fox-hole as he waited for whatever action the enemy might bring him after dark.

All of their underground survival systems were primitive but functional enough to support a huge underground population. What is even more striking is that their support systems such as ventilation were so well hidden that had we known where they were we could have taken them out quickly.

It was highly critical that any success they expected to have depended upon the fact that their small trapdoors were made to be virtually invisible. After the war tourists from all over the world came to marvel at these secret underground mazes which were now being touted as tourist attractions. One Vietnamese guide often has his tourists stand in a circle about 20 feet in diameter and challenges anyone to find the tunnel trapdoor that is within that area. No one ever does. The tunnel guide stamps his foot on the ground and a grinning confederate lifts the trap door and pops out like a Jack-in-a-box. That's him on this book's cover!

You have to admire the cleverly engineered system with its secret trap doors leading down into multiple tunnel levels. This is a tribute to those who built them that enabled their people to live underground virtually for years because the extremely rudimentary life support systems they had worked. Only with careful knife or bayonet probing were our forces able to detect these well-hidden trap doors. As I described earlier the inhabitants took care to make sure that whatever camouflage their trap doors had it blended in with its surroundings. They encouraged plants to grow atop them. If any died showing the presence of brown patches that might look suspicious these were instantly removed and more greenery added.

8

Human Beings Don't Do What I did

Tunnel rats were a special breed. Size alone set them apart from most of their comrades. Necessity to fit into the tunnels meant that they had to be smaller than the average-sized American. They specialized in the most dangerous kind of warfare that took place underground and in total darkness. An effort was made to train some of our South Vietnamese military forces for this job but it failed miserably. None of them wanted to go there. They knew the dangers. Those who went made a habit of quickly re-appearing to claim that the tunnel was short and no one was there. Who could blame them?

Other tunnel rats that went down never came out in one piece. The enemy was sometimes there in the darkness; their eyes already adapted to seeing well. The instant someone came down they were either garroted or had their throats cut by an enemy waiting for them. That's why the usual practice when a tunnel was found was to toss in a grenade and let it do its job. That was exactly what the enemy hoped and intended would happen with their zigzag tunnel plan. Our troops above figured they had taken care of the situation and the enemy troops below went on with their covert plans. Neither one wanted any more contact with the other. Both knew there would be a time and a place for contact.

That's why the real tunnel rats were guys sharp enough to know what might be down there and how they planned to handle it. The good ones were always on hair-trigger. In the darkness they developed sixth senses as to whether they were alone or not down there. Smell was one of the giveaways that the enemy might be awaiting them in the darkness. A whiff of fish was an instant alert because that was part of the enemy soldiers' diet – smelly fish and rice.

Successful tunnel rats were well aware that unlike all the other grunts in their fire teams the rat was a loner whose reward was the satisfaction in knowing that he took on missions no other soldier could tackle. Some of these guys were deeply troubled aggressive personalities who discovered their true selves in the tunnels. Others were normal well-balanced personalities who volunteered for the job because of their smaller size. They often were the ones who came out of the service with intensely scarred memories and nightmares that they lived and re-lived for years. Most simply could not tell their loved ones about the horrors they had seen and done.

One of the 1966 tunnel rats later revealed that each time he went down into a tunnel he felt fear like he had never felt fear before. He said, "I was just an animal. We were all animals. We were dogs, we were snakes; we were dirt pigs. We weren't human beings. Human beings don't do the things we did. I was a killer rat with poisoned teeth. I was trained to kill and I killed. Looking back it's unreal. Unnatural. It's almost like someone else did it. It wasn't really me, because I wouldn't even think of doing anything close to that again."

This fellow was seriously wounded by a mine, then hospitalized and repatriated. For years he suffered with nightmares like most tunnel rats. He didn't talk to anyone about his experiences for at least ten years. Only much later in life did he ever reveal those nightmares and often-painful experiences.

Beside the possibility of the enemy hiding in the tunnel there was the continual fear of blowing yourself up with hidden mines or tunnel booby traps. The simplest of all was an artillery shell – one of our duds – that the enemy rejuvenated, and then dug down into a hole below ground level so that a person's weight pressed the shell down on a sharp projection that fired the cap and triggered the detonation.

The VC was quick to recover any of our duds – bombs, cartridges, grenades or shells. The enemy devoted underground factories to re-packaging the explosive elements of these failing-to-fire items into crude but effective mines and booby traps that were used against us; especially in the tunnels.

In one case a regimental battalion commander stepped on a booby-trapped 155-mm shell and the medical report said that there wasn't enough of him left to fill a shopping bag. He had been disintegrated.

The enemy would call this a sophisticated trap but at the other end of the spectrum was a concealed bow with the ends of the bow concealed in the walls of the tunnel. An arrow was placed under tension to the bow and a trip wire at the target area triggered it. Along with this primitive device would be the heavily weighted mud ball containing sharp bamboo stakes sticking out all over it like a pincushion. This was attached to a tree beside a trail under pressure to a powerful vine. When triggered it swung swiftly across the trail impaling whatever unfortunate creature was in its path.

9

Hey, GI, You Lose Fountain Pen?

Every sharp-eyed point man always watched for ways the enemy tried to hide those trip wires. Any leaf or debris on a trail could conceal such a thing. Knowing this, the clever enemy sometimes used a thin vine or sometimes a tree root as a triggering device.

Which of course is why our troops avoided moving along any trails; choosing instead the far less likely overgrown areas under the jungle canopy.

But in the tunnels you had no such option. Where it went, the rat went, more often in the dark by feel alone!

Booby traps might be anywhere. One report was of finding a storage room underground for nothing but large bags of rice. It was one of the enemy's food storage areas. Tunnel rats early on learned that these bags of rice sometimes concealed other things such as important documents and maps, so they were often opened and the searcher's arm thrust down feeling for other goodies hidden in the rice.

The enemy knew this. So they sometimes included a small booby trap surprise for the searcher. Like a box of Crackerjack with a surprise in it. The single most bizarre booby trap I ever heard that was found in a bag of rice was this: *A Parker 51 pen*. The tiny device was made to explode but whether or not it did is unknown. Like fancy looking Swiss watches offered by the Black Market during WW2, it was a counterfeit. Only difference: this one was deadly. This one was intended to explode when picked up.

Some readers might not know what a Parker 51 pen was.

During World War II that marvelous miniature-writing device known as the Parker 51 fountain pen was the "Rolex" of the sharp-pointed pens that wrote with ink. Apparently the enemy thought it was something still popular enough to catch a GI's eye in the Vietnam War. Imagine if that had not been found by a tunnel rat but later was spotted by a VC opening that bag of rice for a meal. Hopefully he would recognize it for what it was. No rice farmer ever lost such a thing as that. Otherwise this scenario might have gone like this:

"Hey, Fang, look what someone lost in the rice … **Kaboom!**

In time the Americans came up with some shrewd ideas about how to find the hidden tunnels. Especially in areas where they were known to have a dense network of them underground. What they did was bulldoze a large area free of vegetation, then drag trees around that huge clearing until all you saw was smooth ground.

By the next morning when the officers viewed this clearing they quickly saw where the nighttime underground inhabitants had emerged and went to and from the various hidden entrances. The clearing revealed a lot to those who were destroying the tunnels as quickly as they could find them.

10

Those Tunnels Today

Today, some of Vietnam's incredible tunnel systems are major tourist attractions especially those at Cu Chi. A 75-mile long complex of tunnels there were preserved by the Vietnam government as a war memorial. Two different tunnel display sites, one at Ben Dinh and Ben Duoc were set aside and in some cases tunnels were enlarged so that visitors could enter them and visit some of the safer parts of the system. Both sites display dim lights so that guests can see details of the tunnels. Both have displays of booby traps that were used. And in one case, visitors have reconstructed the underground conference rooms where the Tet Offensive was planned in 1968. These have been restored. Visitors may also enjoy a simple meal of the food the Viet Cong fighters would have eaten.

Above ground vendors sell souvenirs and there is a shooting range where visitors can fire assault rifles such as the M-16, the AK-47 and the M-60 machine-gun.

Tourists are also interested in a complex of tunnels called the Vinh Moc tunnels in Quang Tri, Vietnam. During the war it was a strategic area on the border of North Vietnam and South Vietnam. The tunnels were built to shelter people from the intense bombing that was being targeted in that area. The American forces believed the villagers of Vinh Moc were supplying food and armaments to the North Vietnamese garrison there. The idea was to force the villagers to leave the area. But since there was no place in Vietnam for them to go, they dug the tunnels and moved the village 30 feet underground.

The Americans then designed bombs that would go down 30 feet. Faced with these odds the villagers dug down a distance of 60 feet where they established their village in those tunnels. Several stages of this system were developed in 1966 and used until early 1972. This complex included wells, kitchens, rooms for each family, and spaces for health care. Sixty families lived in the tunnels and as many as 17 children were born there.

The tunnels were a huge success and no villagers lost their lives. The only direct hit was from a bomb that failed to explode. The resulting hole was used by the underground population as a ventilation shaft.

History will note that the war took place in Vinh Moc from 1966 to 1972 when the U.S. Army dropped over 9,000 tons of bombs on the area with the ratio of 7 tons of bombs on the average per person. The locals began to dig tunnels in 1965 and finished in 1967. Using simple tools it took them 2,160 days of hard labor. The tunnels are on three levels totaling over a mile long with six entrances to the top of hills and seven entrances to the South China Sea.

Today this tourist attraction can be visited by organized tours and is regularly included in four-day trips from Quay to exploration of the DMZ. In comparison to the Cu Chi tunnels further south, walking through the Vinh Moc tunnels is a lot more comfortable because they are situated in a less humid climate zone. Also the height of the tunnels allows even Western people to stand upright.

ABOUT THE AUTHOR

Author Robert F. Burgess grew up in Grand Rapids, Michigan. He joined the Regular Army in 1946 and qualified as an Expert on the M1 Garand Rifle. As a member of the 88th Division Ski Troops the Germans called "The Blue Devils" he was stationed in the Italian Alps. Later his outfit became TRUST, the Trieste U.S. Troops occupying Trieste on the Adriatic. His garrison stopped Marshal Tito's Yugoslavian Army from taking that disputed territory which was later given to Italy.

Bob lives in north Florida where he writes fast-paced adventure books that put readers up front in the action. Click this link for his Amazon book page and sample the action: **http://www.amazon.com/Robert-F-Burgess/e/B002ZHF0PQ**

A heavily illustrated Kindle e-book that covers all of his major adventures is *Sailing to Adventure: The Time of Our Lives* at **http://www.amazon.com/dp/B00GQKOM2U**

Made in the USA
Middletown, DE
07 February 2022

60729364R00106